WHAT MAKES LAW

This book offers an advanced introduction to central questions in legal philosophy. What factors determine the content of the law in force? What makes a normative system a legal system? How does law beyond the state differ from domestic law? What kind of moral force does law have? These are all questions about the nature of law. The most important existing views are introduced, but the aim is not to survey the existing literature. Rather, this book introduces the subject by stepping back from the fray to sketch the big picture, to show just what is at stake in these old debates.

Legal philosophy has become somewhat arid and inward looking. In part this is because the disagreement between the main camps on the important questions is apparently intractable. The main aim of this book is to suggest both a diagnosis and a proper practical response to this situation of intractable disagreement about questions that do matter.

Liam Murphy works in legal, moral, and political philosophy and the application of these inquiries to law and legal theory. He has published two books: *Moral Demands in Nonideal Theory* (2000) and *The Myth of Ownership: Taxes and Justice* (2002, with Thomas Nagel). His articles have appeared in *Philosophy & Public Affairs* among other journals. Murphy has been an associate editor and now is a member of the editorial board of *Philosophy & Public Affairs*. He is Herbert Peterfreund Professor of Law and Professor of Philosophy at New York University.

CAMBRIDGE INTRODUCTIONS TO PHILOSOPHY AND LAW

Series Editors

Brian H. Bix
University of Minnesota
William A. Edmundson
Georgia State University

This introductory series of books provides concise studies of the philosoph-ical foundations of law, of perennial topics in the philosophy of law, and of important and opposing schools of thought. The series is aimed principally at students in philosophy, law, and political science.

Matthew Kramer, *Objectivity and the Rule of Law*
Larry Alexander and Emily Sherwin, *Demystifying Legal Reasoning*
Larry Alexander, Kimberly Kessler Ferzan, and Stephen J. Morse, *Crime and Culpability*
William A. Edmundson, *An Introduction to Rights*, 2nd edition
Robin West, *Normative Jurisprudence*
Gregory S. Alexander and Eduardo S. Penalver, *An Introduction to Property Theory*
Brian H. Bix, *Contract Law*
Pablo E. Navarro and Jorge L. Rodriguez, *Deontic Logic and Legal Systems*

What Makes Law

AN INTRODUCTION TO THE PHILOSOPHY OF LAW

Liam Murphy

New York University

CAMBRIDGE
UNIVERSITY PRESS

CAMBRIDGE
UNIVERSITY PRESS

32 Avenue of the Americas, New York, NY 10013-2473, USA

Cambridge University Press is part of the University of Cambridge.

It furthers the University's mission by disseminating knowledge in the pursuit of
education, learning, and research at the highest international levels of excellence.

www.cambridge.org
Information on this title: www.cambridge.org/9780521542197

First published 2014

Printed in the United States of America

A catalog record for this publication is available from the British Library.

Library of Congress Cataloging in Publication data
Murphy, Liam B., 1960– author.
What makes law : an introduction to the philosophy of law / Liam Murphy.
    pages   cm – (Cambridge introductions to philosophy and law)
Includes bibliographical references and index.
ISBN 978-0-521-83427-8 (hardback) – ISBN 978-0-521-54219-7 (paperback)
1. Law – Philosophy.   2. Jurisprudence.   I. Title.
K231.M88   2014
340′.1–dc23   2013048833

ISBN 978-0-521-83427-8 Hardback
ISBN 978-0-521-54219-7 Paperback

For Sibylle

Contents

Acknowledgments

I have been thinking and teaching about the issues in this book for about twenty years. Over that period my views have changed a lot. Throughout I have benefited enormously from countless conversations with Lewis Kornhauser, who generously discussed each new idea with me. His skepticism about the very issue of the nature of law has been one of the main influences on this book. I have also benefited greatly over the years from discussions with my students at the NYU School of Law.

Over the ten years or so I have been working on the book, very many others have helped me. I am grateful to colleagues and audience members at Columbia University; Harvard University; London School of Economics; New York University; Pontifical Catholic University, Rio de Janeiro; Princeton University; Queens University; Stanford University; The University of California, Berkeley; The University of California, Los Angeles; The University of Melbourne; The University of Texas, Austin; The University of Toronto; The University of Vienna; The University of Warwick; University College London; and Yale University. Some of the people whose comments and conversation have influenced my thinking the most are: Daniel Baker, Gabriella Blum, Tom Campbell, David Chalmers, David Dyzenhaus, Sibylle Fischer, Barbara Fried, David Golove, Leslie Green, Mark Greenberg, Paul Horwich, Robert Howse, Muhammad Ali Khalidi, Benedict Kingsbury, Nicola Lacey, Joseph Raz, Kristen Rundle, Lawrence Sager, T. M. Scanlon, Frederick Schauer, Samuel Scheffler, Stefan Sciaraffa, Seana Shiffrin, Nicos Stavropoulos,

Jeremy Waldron, Wil Waluchow, and Moran Yahav. Special mention must be made of Ronald Dworkin and Thomas Nagel, who kept inviting me back to the NYU Colloquium in Legal, Political, and Social Philosophy for yet another patient and friendly demonstration that whatever it was I wanted to do, which was not at all clear, I had not yet got it right. The pervasive influence of the writings of Joseph Raz will be obvious from the steady drumbeat of citations from start to finish. Most recently I have benefited from excellent comments on the whole manuscript by the series editors, William A. Edmundson and Brian H. Bix. On top of that, I owe Bill and Brian and a long series of editors at Cambridge University Press huge gratitude for their cheerful patience as the years went by. Sibylle Fischer found me a title one night while driving on NY Route 17. Erick Rabin and Moran Yahav provided excellent and generous research assistance. Finally, the support of the Filomen D'Agostino and Max E. Greenberg Research Fund of New York University School of Law is gratefully acknowledged.

1   Introduction

> *Philosopher*: We have hitherto spoken of Laws without considering
> any thing of the Nature and Essence of a Law; and now unless we
> define the word Law, we can go no farther without Ambiguity, and
> Fallacy, which will be but loss of time; whereas, on the contrary,
> the Agreement upon our words will enlighten all we have to say
> hereafter.
>
> *Lawyer*: I do not remember the Definition of Law in any Statute.
> $\qquad\qquad\qquad\qquad\qquad\qquad\qquad$ (Hobbes [1681] 1971, 69)

Different kinds of philosophical questions can be asked about law. John
Rawls's major works (1996, 1999) can be seen as treatises on what the
content of law should be if a state is to be both legitimate and just. Other
inquiries lie more clearly within legal theory in that they evaluate different ways of designing the kind of governance structure we call law
(Kornhauser 2004): Should we prefer formally realizable legal rules
(Kennedy 1976), or more open standards? What principles must legal
rules or standards satisfy to realize the moral ideal of the rule of law, and
thus govern us appropriately as responsible agents?

Though this book touches on such questions, this is usually to contrast them with my main topic, which is the nature of law. There are two
main questions, though my focus is overwhelmingly on the first of them.
When we ask what makes law, we may have in mind the question of how
we determine the content of the law in force. This is the question of the
grounds of law. The ancient issue here – though it has become a major

1

concern of philosophy only over the past two hundred years or so – is
whether moral considerations are ever relevant when we are trying to
find out what the law is, as opposed to what it ought to be. The other
question we may have in mind, which I will not reach until the end of
this book, is that of what makes a normative order an order of law, rather
than something else, such as conventional morality, or etiquette, or a code
of honor among thieves.

Of the two main parties on the issue of the grounds of law, those who
deny that moral considerations are always relevant when figuring out the
content of law go by the name of "positivists." The opposing camp, which
holds that moral considerations are always relevant, has lacked an appropriate name – so I just call it "nonpositivism." An enormous amount has
been written about this debate since H. L. A. Hart first published *The
Concept of Law* in 1961 (Hart 1994), and especially since Ronald Dworkin
began his attack on positivism in his article "The Model of Rules" in 1967
(in Dworkin 1978). The next three chapters of this book aim to lay out
the bare bones of this debate. It is not my intention to do justice to its
many twists and turns. Rather, I hope to motivate the two positions, to
explain what each side most fundamentally believes, and to present their
positions in what seems to me to be their most favorable light. This will
mean ignoring many complications and, on occasion, helping myself to
revisionist interpretations of the main texts.

Chapter 2 explains the crucial difference between a theory of what
makes the content of law what it is – the issue of the grounds of law – and
a theory of how judges and other legal decision makers should decide
cases. Understanding this distinction is crucial to any understanding of
the debate about the grounds of law. I also provide an extremely short
introduction to the two positions and the history of the debate. More
detailed accounts of positivism and nonpositivism are provided in the
following two chapters.

Chapter 3 takes Hart as our paradigm positivist, though reference is
made to the two other most important defenders of this position, Hans
Kelsen and Joseph Raz. It is in my interpretation of Hart that I take

perhaps the greatest liberties, in an attempt to get to what I believe is the most forceful and plausible version of his theory of law; I do not spend very much time discussing the complexities and occasional infelicities of his own text nor much of the voluminous literature about it. Chapter 4 is mostly about the most important nonpositivist philosopher, Ronald Dworkin. Here too I am brief. I unpack Dworkin's position into a number of distinct claims that are, together, a compelling package, but that are not all essential to nonpositivism as I understand it. Nonpositivism is the view that moral considerations are always relevant to determining the content of the law in force. Dworkin believed that, but he believed much else besides, and it is important to understand that one could embrace nonpositivism while disagreeing with some of Dworkin's other claims.

There are many excellent scholarly works about both Hart and Dworkin that are more comprehensive than my two chapters. My aim is to set up two clear and attractive positions so that we can get on with the problem of how we might decide between them.

This is a big problem. One main claim of this book is that the two camps represent two fundamentally opposed visions of the kind of thing law is, and that nothing so much as an argument is likely to move either side closer to the other. As I explain in detail in the core chapter of the book, Chapter 6, I believe that no argument for either side is likely to carry more conviction than the foundational initial stance that each brings to the table. For positivists, law is grounded in fact alone. For nonpositivists, though law connects with social and political fact, it is also in its nature something good, or at least potentially so – so of course morality is relevant when figuring its content. I am unaware of any argument that makes use of premises that don't, in effect, require either side to give up its foundational commitment.

This standoff perhaps sheds light on an often noted feature of the debate about the grounds of law: many lawyers and philosophers believe that it is entirely empty and pointless. That view is on the face of it surprising, since it could only not matter how we determine the content of law if it doesn't matter what the law is. Frustration with the standoff is not itself a good enough reason to dismiss the debate. A serious attack on the importance of the question of the grounds of law requires defending the view we don't, in fact, need to know what the content of the law is. This "eliminativist" option is discussed at length in Chapter 6. But though it must be taken seriously, it must be wrong. There is an important contrast to be drawn between the question what is law and questions about other contested political ideas, such as what is democracy, what is liberty, and what is the rule of law. To set up the contrast, I discuss in Chapter 5 several examples of "What is X?" disputes in political philosophy and reach the conclusion that these debates really don't matter. They don't matter because we can continue to talk about all the political issues that matter to us without agreeing exactly about what, say, democracy *really is*. The case is different for law, because we cannot replace talk about what the content of the law is with talk about something else – such as what judges should do.

The main reason we cannot just forget about the content of law is that, depending on the legal subject, there is often strong moral reason to comply with it. Chapter 7 discusses the old question of whether there is a standing (but overridable) moral duty to follow the law. The position I defend is instrumental, or consequentialist – people should follow the law when this will do more good than some alternative action. This means that for private individuals compliance with law will frequently not be morally required. But – and this is the main claim of the chapter – I believe that government officials, especially high-ranking officials, typically have very strong moral reasons to comply. Coupled with the argument in Chapter 8 that states, especially powerful states, typically have strong moral reasons to comply with international law, this amounts to the position that "law for states" (Goldsmith & Levinson 2009) matters greatly, and provides the main reason the whole issue of the grounds of law is important.

My two conclusions, that law (especially for states) matters, but that opposing views about how to figure out the content of the law seem to be intractable to argument, leave me with a problem. If the content of law matters so much, and the two views reflect fundamentally different strongly held views, how is it that so many lawyers, politicians, and ordinary people are not at all concerned about the debate between positivism and nonpositivism? If we have to know which view is right before we can know the content of the law, and if the content of the law matters, why aren't we all arguing about this problem all the time? The answer to this question, I argue in Chapter 6, is that the two views overlap considerably in the direction they give us about how to figure out the content of law. Though one side says morality is never relevant and the other side says it always is, this fundamental disagreement is frequently not engaged. So, though in many cases the different views will yield different answers to the question of what the law around here is, in many more cases they will not. My concluding chapter offers some brief thoughts about how much we should be concerned about the cases where the two views yield different conclusions.

The second main question about the nature of law, what makes law law rather than something else, is discussed in Chapter 8. That chapter surveys several issues that international law and other forms of law beyond the state raise, including how positivist and nonpositivist views play out in that domain. But the main focus is on the questions of whether international law qualifies as a legal system and whether law beyond the state can be thought of as a form of law at all – rather than, say, conventional morality among global actors. In discussing this latter issue, I venture a view. While the availability of coercive enforcement cannot be seen as a necessary condition for a normative order counting as a legal order, I do believe that when it is law we are talking about (rather than, say, morality or etiquette), we hold that coercive enforcement is in principle appropriate. In venturing a view that I hope might be compelling to any reader, I here show that I do not believe that disagreements about what makes law law reflect the kind of foundational standoff we see with the issue of the grounds of law. But of course I may be wrong about that.

2 Morality and the Grounds of Law

Adjudication and the Grounds of Law

The main traditional dispute about the nature of law, and the one that is the main focus of this book, is a dispute about what morality has to do with figuring out the content of the law in force in any particular place.

On the one hand we have matters of fact, such as the meaning of what is written in some document that is issued by some legal institution such as a legislature. On the other hand we have moral considerations, in the broad sense that includes not just individual right and wrong but also normative political theory (about, say, social justice or the proper limits of state power). Everyone thinks that matters of fact are relevant to determining the content of current law. The main dispute about the nature of law is a dispute about whether moral considerations are also relevant. This is a dispute about what Dworkin (1986, 4) called the grounds of law – of what makes legal propositions true.

This dispute is obviously distinct from the question of whether moral judgment does or should influence those who make law. We can take for granted that it should and to some extent does. The question is whether moral considerations are relevant to figuring out what the law already is.

What may not be so obvious is that the issue of the grounds of law is also distinct from that of whether judges should appeal to moral considerations when adjudicating disputes. Explaining this contrast is perhaps the best way to bring the traditional debate about the grounds of law into focus.

Any government official whose role it is to determine the legal rights and duties of others requires a theory of legal decision making. In the case of judges, we call this a theory of adjudication. Officials from other branches of government also make decisions about the legal rights and duties of others, which will be important in later chapters, but judges provide the central case and the natural place to start.

A judge's theory of adjudication may be sketchy and perhaps only implicitly believed, but she must have one. Decisions about people's legal situations obviously cannot be made without having views about which considerations it is appropriate to take into account. It is not essential, by contrast, that judges have a theory of the grounds of law – a theory that would tell them whether and when moral considerations are relevant to the question of what the law (already) is.

A record of the reasoning behind a judicial decision may cite many factors that were thought to be relevant, such as the contents of constitutions, statutes, prior judicial opinions, the prevailing custom in a particular industry or place, the opinions of legal scholars, and considerations of social welfare, justice, and fairness. A judicial opinion (in common-law jurisdictions, at any rate) explains how and why a decision was reached, and therefore tells us a lot about the judge's theory of adjudication, but it will not necessarily reveal her views about which of the factors on which the decision was based were part of already existing law.

If judges were called on always to announce the state of the prior law as they found it, they would need to reveal their views, for example, about whether considerations of fairness are part of the law or rather fall into the category of considerations not part of law that are nonetheless legitimately taken into account in adjudication. Such categorization requires a theory about which kinds of factors are, in principle, relevant to figuring out the content of the law; it requires a theory of the grounds of law. It is typically not necessary for judges to engage in such categorization, and so it is typically not necessary for judges to have a theory of the grounds of law.

This holds true even when common-law courts explicitly "overrule" or "decline to follow" a precedent. Such a statement leaves open whether the discredited precedent was, in the view of the court, formerly part of the law, which is now changed, or instead a mistake that was never part of the law properly understood. Both views are found in traditional common-law thinking, but judges working within the common law need not take a stand.

Some judges and some legal theorists believe that all normative considerations that judges are authorized to take into account when deciding a case are necessarily part of the existing law. We can call this the adjudicatory or adjudicative (Perry 1987) view of law. The implication of the adjudicatory view is that there is no interesting gap between determining what the law is and marshaling the considerations relevant to resolving a particular dispute before a court.[1] If the adjudicatory view of law is correct, then it is misleading to say that it is not necessary for judges to have a theory of the grounds of law. But the adjudicatory view of law may or may not be correct, and it is not necessary for judges to have a view about whether it is.

The majority and the dissent in the nineteenth-century New York case *Riggs v. Palmer*[2] disagreed about statutory interpretation. Francis Palmer's will, formally valid under the relevant statutes in New York State, left his estate to the person who murdered him. The majority argued for the relevance of the fact that the legislature, had it ever considered such a case, would never have intended to allow a murdering heir to inherit. It also argued that statutes should be interpreted in light of "fundamental

---

[1] There will still be a gap, on any plausible view: mathematics and logic can help determine the outcome of a legal dispute, but no one believes that they are part of the law in force. The terms of a contract will in part determine the outcome of a contract dispute. It seems natural not to regard those terms as part of existing law, but some may prefer to talk that way – to treat the contract as private legislation between the parties. But this is not an interesting disagreement. What matters is whether the normative considerations of fairness, justice, and the rest are, if legitimately appealed to in adjudication, therefore part of the law in force.

[2] 115 N.Y. 506 (1889).

maxims of the common law." The dissenting judges argued for a straight-forward application of the literal meaning of the words of the relevant statutes. Dworkin characterizes this dispute as one "about what the law was, about what the real statute the legislators enacted really said" (1986, 20). But while the judges clearly disagreed about proper adjudication, we simply do not know whether they all embraced the theory of the grounds of law according to which all normative factors legitimately taken into account in adjudication are at the same time relevant to determining the content of the existing law. They did not say. They did not take a stand on the nature of law because it was not necessary.

It is sometimes claimed that all, or almost all, judges hold the adjudicatory view of law. If this were true, it would provide some support for it. But the evidence does not support the claim. In the United States, prominent and scholarly judges who have addressed the issue – from Oliver Wendell Holmes Jr. to Learned Hand to Richard Posner – have thought it obvious that judges must, on occasion and under constraint, "legislate."[3] Benjamin Cardozo (1921) elaborated a theory for such legislative adjudication – using what he called the "method of sociology," a judge should fill gaps in the existing law with recourse to community morality. Most judges, however, neither announce their theory of law in their opinions nor write books or articles about the judicial process, so it is hard to know what theory of law they hold.

It is true that in recent times it has become typical for judges and aspiring judges in the United States publicly to disavow "legislating from the bench." But many of these same judges would equally adamantly deny that applying the law ever requires them to have recourse to "their own" moral or political views. As it would precisely be inclusion of moral judgment within the bounds of law that would give existing law the resources

---

[3] "I recognize without hesitation that judges do and must legislate, but they can do so only interstitially; they are confined from molar to molecular motions." *Southern Pacific Co. v. Jensen*, 244 U.S. 205, 221 (1917, Holmes, J., dissenting). Hand (1952) takes a similar view, as does Posner (2008, 81–92).

to generate an answer to all questions before a court, this makes it a little mysterious just what theory of law these judges hold.[4]

Of course there is this truth in what most judges say: whatever else is controversial in the theory of adjudication, judges ought to apply the law. Is the upshot that even if applying the law is not all that judges must do, they nevertheless will need a theory of law – that this is in fact the primary thing that they do need (Dworkin 2006, 18–21)?

It is true that one way to develop a theory of adjudication is to start with a theory of the grounds of law and only later turn to the issues of when judges may depart from prior law (if the theory of the grounds of law makes that ever seem necessary) and of how decisions should be made when valid law does not settle the issue (if the theory of the grounds of law makes that a possibility). But it is also possible to start from the immediate practical question of how to decide a

---

[4] It is a commonplace of jurisprudence – that no theorist or judge could really disagree with – that a literal reading of legal sources will not in itself yield answers to all legal questions. Though some legal systems or areas of law are more or less determinate than others, there will always be cases where a reasonable reading of the materials could go either way. There may or may not be a method of adjudication, such as "originalism" or Cardozo's method of sociology, that could allow a judge to supplement the guidance of legal sources without reference to her own moral or political judgment. (That seems dubious, but it is not our topic here.) But even if one were available in principle, there is no consensus (in most jurisdictions) that any such method is mandated by existing legal sources, read plain. It is quite appropriate, then, that Justice Antonin Scalia of the U.S. Supreme Court defends originalism on political grounds (Scalia 1998), just as Cardozo before him defended the method of sociology. Both hold that judges should appeal to other material when they need more guidance than the legal sources can give them; both hold that this other material should be something other than a judge's own moral convictions, something more objective. But neither holds that his preferred method of adjudication is mandated by existing law. To be a good judge, even on these approaches, you need to reach the right moral conclusion about how to make decisions on your own; no legal authority is directing you in this matter. In the face of its evident absurdity, the pervasive contemporary disavowal of the need for moral reasoning on the part of judges, at least in the United States, is something of a political pathology that is itself worthy of investigation. For an extended discussion, see Kennedy (1998). The current point, however, is simply that in this political environment we would be unwise to treat what judges say about the nature of law at face value.

case.[5] And if we start from that end, there is no need, within the theory of adjudication, to mark the boundary between law and not law.

There have been exceptional cases where courts have declared that a decision about the content of prior law was necessary to resolve a legal dispute. Shortly after the reunification of Germany, two former East German border guards were convicted of homicide for the shooting of a person attempting to climb the Berlin Wall. The guards appealed, in part on the ground that the shooting was in accordance with the law of the former German Democratic Republic: the killing was therefore justified by law in force at the time, and so the homicide convictions must be seen as retroactive criminalization that violated the constitution of the now unified Federal Republic of Germany. The appellate court, the Criminal Division of the German Federal Court of Justice, agreed that the convictions would have been unconstitutional if the killings had been in accordance with valid East German law. But there was no retroactivity, the court held, because the legislation of the German Democratic Republic that regulated the policing of the border was, in virtue of its grossly unjust content (authorizing guards to shoot at people fleeing over the border), no law at all.[6]

In this case the court made a statement about the grounds of law. It was moved to do so presumably because it seemed that there was no other way it could uphold the convictions in the face of the potentially justifying legislation. In support of its declaration that grossly unjust law was not law at all, it cited a 1946 article by Gustav Radbruch (2006) published in a German law journal. There was, however, a less adventurous route to the same outcome. Reviewing a similar set of convictions, the German Constitutional Court, while not impugning the constitutionality of the approach of the Federal Court of Justice, showed how the

---

[5] Here is how Posner sees it: "A judge does not reach a point in a difficult case at which he says, 'The law has run out and now I must do some legislating.' He knows that he has to decide and that whatever he does decide will (within the broadest of limits) be law; for the judge as occasional legislator is still a judge" (2008, 85).

[6] BGHSt 39, 1 (1992).

convictions could be upheld without taking a stand on the grounds of law.[7] The Constitutional Court upheld homicide convictions stemming from shootings at the wall on the basis of a creative interpretation of the constitutional ban on retroactivity. Article 103(2) of the German Constitution holds that "An act may be punished only if it was defined by a law as a criminal offense before the act was committed."[8] This, the court held, did not apply to a situation where an otherwise criminal act was justified by a grossly unjust law. The court justified this interpretation with an argument about the point of having a ban on retroactive punishment in a democratic society. Approaching the issue in this way, the court avoided having to pronounce on the validity of the legislation governing the activities of the border guards at the time of the shooting and so avoided having to take a stand on whether morality was relevant to the determination of the content of the law.

The German Constitutional Court in this case certainly engaged in moral reasoning along the way to reaching its decision. Suppose we think that this was entirely appropriate. That would indicate nothing about our view on whether moral considerations are relevant to determining the content of the law. One excellent way to characterize what legal philosophers have been disagreeing about is precisely this question: When a conscientious judge appropriately appeals to moral considerations to reach a decision, has he in so doing gone beyond the mere application of existing law and in part also made new law? One side says yes, its opponents no. The dispute about the grounds of law is not about what judges should do, but you could say it is about the correct description of what they do.[9]

Once this becomes clear, however, many start to wonder why anyone ever thought this dispute mattered. If judges can do without a theory of

---

[7] BVerfGE 95, 96.

[8] Official translation available at: https://www.btg-bestellservice.de/pdf/80201000.pdf.

[9] "Much of legal theory can be seen as an attempt better to understand what a court takes from the law and what it gives to it, where the application of the law stops and judicial discretion begins, what the boundary is between the law the court finds and the law it creates" (Raz 1986, 1117).

the grounds of law and that theory affects merely how we can describe what judges do, why would anyone bother with it?

The Law in Force

The reason is that anyone who is attempting to answer a question about the content of law must as an initial matter have a view about the grounds of law.

Had a German law professor been asked, prior to the trials of the former border guards, whether the intentional killings at the wall were criminal homicides when they happened, she would not have been able to avoid taking a stand on the grounds of law. If they were not criminal homicides, the justifying East German law (which we can assume was grossly unjust) was valid, and Radbruch's account of the grounds of law is rejected. Suppose that this is the view of our professor. We might next ask her what she thinks about the Constitutional Court's argument that the convictions should stand even if the killings were not crimes at the time. The professor may dodge the question by saying that it was a good decision, that she "agrees" with it. That is multiply ambiguous. She may mean, first, that the court correctly applied German constitutional law as it was prior to its decision. Or she may mean that the court, acting within its legal authority and thus in accordance with law, reinterpreted and thus changed, at least for this case, German constitutional law in a manner she thought wise. Last, she may mean that, even though the court exceeded its legal authority in acting as it did, this was, in the circumstances, the morally right thing to do – taking into account, she might say, the importance of some kind of public accountability for the crimes of the former East German regime. After all, she might add, even though judges are, as a matter of morality, duty bound to act in accordance with law, that duty is not absolute, and sometimes other factors may outweigh it.

To keep things reasonably simple, we can leave aside the issue of whether, and if so when, it is morally appropriate for a judge to make decisions that are not in accordance with law. If we ask our professor to choose between the first and second ways of understanding what she said, we will force her, once again, to take on the issue of the grounds of law. We know that she holds the justifying East German legislation valid. If she believes that the convictions were nonetheless constitutional under the law as it was before the court made its decision, she must believe that the argument of political morality the Constitutional Court engaged in to justify its decision falls within the domain of law. If the professor believes that the convictions were not valid under prior German constitutional law, but that the decision was nonetheless in accordance with law and a good decision, then she believes that while the argument of political morality did not fall within the boundary of law, it was nonetheless a legitimate set of considerations for a judge acting according to law to take into account, and that the court's reasoning was sound.

Consider a very different kind of example. Whether the exclusion of same-sex couples from the institution of marriage in New York was in violation of the state constitution in, say, 1995 depends on the grounds of law. Some people believe that the content of the law is determined entirely by legal sources: statutes, constitutions, judicial opinions, and so on, all interpreted in a fashion that never requires the independent moral judgment of the interpreter. If we take this view, we will probably conclude that the existing legal sources did not determinately settle the legality of same-sex marriage in New York in 1995, and so the matter remained open until the Court of Appeals settled it, in the negative, in the 2006 case of *Hernandez v. Robles*.[10] Subsequently, the Marriage Equality Act of 2011 changed the law. Others believe that the content of the law is determined by the best, the morally best, interpretation of the existing legal materials. If we take this view and also believe that equal protection, properly interpreted, implies equal participation, regardless of sex or sexual orientation, in important social institutions such as marriage, we will have little difficulty in reaching the conclusion that the exclusion of same-sex couples from the institution of marriage in New York violated

[10] 7 N.Y.3d 338, 855 N.E.2d 1 (2006).

the equal protection clause of the New York State Constitution in 1995. We could also conclude that the holding to the contrary in *Hernandez* was a mistake and that the legislation of 2011 recognizing same-sex marriage was strictly speaking unnecessary.

On the one view there was no answer to the legal question before *Hernandez*; after that decision, there was for five years the clear answer that same-sex marriage was not legally available in New York until the New York State Legislature changed the law. On the other view, it has for a long time been contrary to law to exclude same sex-couples from the institution of marriage in New York. Different views of the grounds of law, different conclusions about what the law is. And it does seem to matter, to New York residents at any rate, what the law about marriage in New York is.

Each of us needs to take a stance on the dispute about the grounds of law if we want to be able to offer answers to legal questions. Far from nothing turning on it, it looks as though, as far as the law is concerned, everything turns on it. Of course, if it did not matter what the law is, then the dispute about the grounds of law would not matter. This "eliminativist" attitude to the law, radical though it is, must be taken seriously; I discuss it in Chapter 6.

Law and Morality: A Brief History

Some insist that moral considerations are relevant to figuring out what the law is and others that this is never so; each camp believes that the other misunderstands the nature of law in a fundamental way. But that neither camp is obviously mistaken has been recognized at least since Aristotle.

In the *Rhetoric*, Aristotle distinguishes between the "written law," which is specific to a particular place, and the unwritten "common law," which is the same everywhere and expresses what is just by nature (1373b). He then advises those arguing a lawsuit before an Athenian jury to take advantage of the fact that the law governing the dispute could be thought to be grounded either entirely in the written law, or alternatively in the written law as corrected by the common law. Where the written law is against you, you should argue from the common law, pointing out that the written law does not always "perform the function of law." Where the written law is on your side, you should remind the jury that its job is not to try to be "wiser than the laws" (1375a–1375b). The advice is to lean on one or another way of understanding what kind of thing Athenian law is, depending on which understanding better suits your case.

In language that has been familiar in the West since St. Thomas Aquinas's *Treatise on Law*,[11] we could put Aristotle's point this way. Take for granted the fundamental distinction between the *natural law*, which is a distinctive way of understanding what modern philosophers would call universal morality, and *positive* or *human law*, which is the law that is in force in a particular place. The question then arises of whether the human law in a particular place is determined solely by its written or customary legal sources or whether it is at least in part also determined by the natural law. Aristotle sees that both possible answers to this question about the nature of (human) law can be made to seem plausible.

Aquinas perhaps agreed; he did not take a clear stand on whether the natural law is partly determinative of what the human law is, or instead just an external basis for determining what it ought to be. At the start of the *Treatise on Law*, Aquinas writes that all law (human law included) must concern itself with "the happiness of the community." Later, when writing specifically about the human law, he notes that a law is unjust if (among other reasons) it is contrary to the benefit of the community, or imposes unequal burdens, or exceeds the lawmaker's power, and then comments: "These are acts of violence rather than laws, for as Augustine said, 'A law that is unjust is considered no law at all'" (qu. 96). Such remarks suggest the position that conformity with the natural law is always a criterion of validity for the positive law. But other passages suggest the contrary view. The passage just quoted continues: "Therefore laws of this kind do not

[11] *Summa Theologiae*, Qu. 90–7 in Aquinas 1988.

bind in conscience except to avoid scandal or disorder." That suggests that unjust human law still is human law, it is just that the reasons for obeying are not the same as those we have for obeying human law that is in accord with the natural law. This interpretation seems compatible with the statement that if a human law "disagrees in some respect from the natural law, it is no longer a law but a corruption of law." So it is plausible to read Aquinas as allowing unjust human law the status of human law, but refraining from granting it the status of law in the fullest sense of the word, which implies its conformity to the natural law and therefore human reason (Finnis 1996, 2003; I follow Finnis's interpretation).

The important point is that Aquinas seems relatively unconcerned with issues of the validity and interpretation of the human law. Rather, he was concerned with the question of what the human law ought to be and with the nature of the obligation to obey just or unjust rules promulgated by the state, whether they are properly called law or not.

Not until the modern period did legal theorists and philosophers with legal expertise start to offer views on the question of whether morality could or could not be relevant to the determination of what the (positive) law is. Hobbes explicitly states the "command theory" version of legal positivism: law is the command from one person to another who is obliged to obey.[12] But this is not yet positivism in the classical form it took on with Jeremy Bentham in the late eighteenth century, because Hobbes did not believe that the content of the law is one thing, justice or morality another; he believed that there was no such thing as justice without law and so could hardly have allowed that considerations of justice are relevant to the determination of what the law is. Hobbes did hold that the sovereign was subject to the natural law, and that positive law should be interpreted in light of the laws of nature, but as the natural law consists for Hobbes in precepts of rational self-interest, the issue of the relation between positive law and morality is still not joined (see Dyzenhaus 2012 for a contrary interpretation).

---

[12] *Leviathan*, ch. XXVI.

Positivism proper starts with Bentham. More than that, we can say that philosophical discussion of the nature of human law – philosophical discussion of whether, given what kind of thing law is, morality can be a ground of law – starts with Bentham too. It seems that none of the early modern philosophers in the natural law tradition – Suárez, Grotius, Pufendorf, Locke – were any more concerned than Aquinas to take a stand on this question.[13] And neither Hume nor Kant was terribly interested either.[14] Bentham's opponents were not philosophers but theorists of the common law – especially William Blackstone, who was the target of Bentham's first published work, *A Fragment on Government*, in 1776 (see Lieberman 1989; Postema 1986).

Blackstone did appear to take a clear stand on the role of morality in determining the content of the common law. When writing about precedent, and a judge's duty to make decisions based on the existing law rather than his own private judgment, Blackstone commented:

> Yet this rule admits of exceptions, where the former determination is most evidently contrary to reason; much more if it be clearly contrary to the divine law. But even in such cases the subsequent judges do not pretend to make a new law, but to vindicate the old one from misrepresentation. For if it be found that the former decision is manifestly absurd or unjust, it is declared, not that such a sentence was *bad law*; but that it was *not law*; that is, that it is not the established custom of

---

[13] Like Aquinas, Suárez makes remarks that could be interpreted as taking a stand: "The human lawmaker ... does not have the power to bind through unjust laws, and, therefore, were he to command unjust things, such prescriptions would not be law, because they have neither the force nor the validity necessary to bind." "For a law to be genuine law, it must ... be just and reasonable, because an unjust law is not law." Both passages are from *De legibus*, and are cited in Garzón Valdés 1998, 267. Garzón Valdés reads these passages as implying a view that there is no such thing as an unjust human law. They can be read that way, though Suárez in other respects, such as his embrace of the command theory of law (Postema 2012), suggests a reading like Finnis's reading of Aquinas that I embrace in the text. It seems that, as for Aquinas, the important upshot of a "law" being unjust for Suárez is that it does not "bind."

[14] Waldron (1996) plausibly argues that Kant was a legal positivist, but this has to be extracted from the text by way of implication.

the realm, as has been erroneously determined. And hence it is that our lawyers are with justice so copious in their encomiums on the reason of the common law; that they tell us, that the law is the perfection of reason, that it always intends to conform thereto, and that what is not reason is not law. (*Commentaries*, 1: 69–70)

This sounds like the view that an unjust law is an impossibility; if it is unjust, it cannot be law. In the past century or so, many people have used the label "natural law" for that view. But it is doubtful whether anyone ever held such a view. We have seen that Aquinas most probably did not, and the thought that Blackstone did is contradicted by several passages where he rather clearly acknowledges the possibility of unjust law (see Finnis 1967). It is more plausible to read Blackstone as advancing the more subtle and plausible claim that determination of the common law involves the application of reason, understood to include moral judgment, and that on occasion this will justify treating certain (though not all) past decisions as mistakes, and so not part of the body of decisions that are "evidence of what is common law."[15] On this reading, Blackstone's non-positivism was something rather close to Dworkin's theory of law, according to which the content of the law is determined via an interpretation, guided by moral judgment, of existing legal materials.[16]

Bentham confronted this idea of law with a definition of law as the command of a sovereign supported by the threat of a sanction (Bentham 1970; see Postema 1986, chap. 9; 2011). This account of law received its most widely read presentation in John Austin's *The Province of Jurisprudence Determined*, first published in 1832. By the time the fifth edition of this book was published in 1885, debate among philosophers

---

[15] "So that *the law* and the *opinion of the judge*, are not always convertible terms, or one and the same thing; since it sometimes may happen that the judge may *mistake* the law. Upon the whole, however we may take it as a general rule, 'that the decisions of the courts of justice are the evidence of what is common law'" (1: 71). For discussion, see Lieberman 1989, Part I.

[16] On the affinity between traditional common-law theory and Dworkin's views, see Perry 1987.

and lawyers about the relation between law and morality was wide-spread throughout Europe, with positivism in the ascendance, at least in England. Bentham's insistence on the distinction between what the law is and what it ought to be could be described, as early as 1877, and by no less careful and fair-minded a writer than Henry Sidgwick, as "to us so obvious a truism that it seems pedantic to state it expressly" (2000, 207). In Germany, by contrast, the merits of positivism – usually in the guise of "statutory positivism" – remained a matter of contentious debate in the nineteenth century and would become politically explosive during the Weimar period (see Dyzenhaus 1997; Paulson 2006).

In any event, not until the twentieth century were significant philo-sophical contributions to the debate about the nature of law made, particularly through the work of Hans Kelsen, H. L. A. Hart, Ronald Dworkin, and Joseph Raz.

Two Pictures

The most fundamental divide within the debate over the grounds of law is between those who believe that the foundations of the law in a particular place are exclusively matters of fact and those who believe, to the contrary, that the content of the law is also partly a moral matter. Different views within each camp differ on the way factual or moral considerations determine the content of law. These differences, though very important, are downstream of that more fundamental disagreement. The core idea of positivism, then, is that it is in the very nature of law, wherever it is found, that the final determinants of its content are facts, not norms (Coleman 2001a, 75). The opposing view has lacked an appropriate name, which is perhaps why "natural law" has misleadingly been used. "Legal moralism" would also be misleading, as it already has a place in a different debate about the legitimacy of the legal enforcement of morality for its own sake. Dworkin's label "law as integrity" would not do because we are looking for a name for the broader class of views of which Dworkin's is not the only example (though it is by far the most fully developed and the most important). This leaves "nonpositivism." It may seem too broad a label, since to deny that the law is determined just by social facts is not, strictly, to say that it is in part determined by moral considerations in particular. But when we limit ourselves to plausible views, there is no third class of considerations that might be relevant to the content of law: it is either social facts alone or social facts along with moral considerations, especially those of political morality, so it is clear enough what "nonpositivism" means.

In the next two chapters, I try to motivate each of these pictures of what law is, and discuss some of the main internal issues within each camp.

3 Legal Positivism

A Normative System Grounded in Facts

To bring out what motivates positivism, it is best to think of it first in its purest and most plausible version, according to which moral reasoning is never required or appropriate in figuring out what the law is, even if legal sources can be interpreted as calling for it.[1] Legal argument on this view is never, in any part, about what ought to be, never involves thinking about right and wrong, fairness or justice. Of course the language lawyers use overlaps with that used in moral discussion – in both domains we talk of rights, duties, obligations, wrongs, and so forth. But that is no embarrassment to the positivist, who can accept that the law typically and ideally reflects someone or some collective's moral conclusions about what the law should be. Moreover, a statute or constitution or a history of decisions might give a great deal of guidance about what the specifically legal meaning some moral term, such as "justice," may have acquired. What is important is that while the content of the law may have been, and ideally would have been, arrived at after moral deliberation, and while the law may use words also used in moral argument, moral deliberation is not required to identify law's content after it has been made.

The law is what is posited, or put forward by a person or people. We may all hope that what gets posited is good, that it matches closely with

---

[1] This has come to be known as "hard" or "exclusive" positivism; I discuss the "soft" or "inclusive" alternative later in this chapter.

what the law ought, morally speaking, to be. But, insists the positivist, it would be simply mad to look at what *has* been put forward as law by people and see there, instead, what *ought* to have been put forward. Suppose someone were to argue that slavery is illegal in a particular place in part because it is a violation of people's moral rights. The positivist sees such an argument as like defending the claim that sexual promiscuity causes disease by saying that promiscuity deserves to be punished.

Sometimes positivism has been confused with the peculiar view that it is a matter of moral indifference what the content of the law is. In fact, the origins of positivism lie in Bentham's enthusiasm for the reform of law in line with what he took to be the correct account of what it ought to be. One of his concerns was that if people believed it was in the nature of law to be good, this would deter them from subjecting the law to moral critique and then reform (Postema 1986, 304–5). Bentham also believed that the sole basis for sound critique was the principle of utility; but positivism as a theory of law takes no stand on the appropriate moral theory for evaluation of the law.

Positivism is also compatible with the idea there might be something meritorious about law as such. Perhaps there is no law without a legal system, and perhaps anything that qualifies as a legal system has *some* merit. Perhaps too, there are reasons for thinking that, even though law as such does not necessarily provide reasons for action, it often does (a position I myself defend in Chapter 7). The positivist picture of law does not offer any kind of fully general claim about the lack of necessary connections between morality and law (see Gardner 2001 for a clear statement of this point). The claim it makes about the nature of law is very focused: law is a social phenomenon in the specific sense that its content is always fixed by social facts, and so, in reasoning toward a view about the content of current law, it is never appropriate to take into account considerations of what would be better, of what ought to be.

If our thoughts about what it would be morally better for the law to be cannot at all guide our thinking about what it is, what does guide us? The answer is legal sources: statutes, constitutions, judicial opinions, and so on, all interpreted in a fashion that never requires the independent moral judgment of the interpreter (a classic statement is Raz 1994, 194–221). These are the social facts that ground propositions of law. So a positivist account of law must explain how we are to identify which texts or practices count as legal sources, as well as an account of how they may be interpreted in a morally neutral way. Positivist theory has traditionally been more concerned with the first of these.

The positivist rejects such claims as that materials count as legal sources if it is appropriate, from the point of view of political morality, to treat them as such. A positivist may grant that the best possible justification for coercing people according to certain rules is that the rules were arrived at through a democratic process, but insists that this is not at all relevant to the question of whether legislation is a source of law. If legislation is a legal source, we must be able to identify it as such without entering into questions of justification.

Typically, a particular text counts as part of the legal order in a particular place because another, higher-level legal source tells us so. Thus the validity of administrative orders may be established by appeal to legislation, and the validity of legislation by appeal to a written constitution. As Bentham was perhaps the first to insist, legal sources are generally not identified as valid one by one, but rather form a system (Bentham 2010; see Postema 2012 for discussion). But of course the system is not self-validating; if a highest-level legal norm exists that explains the validity of all lower-level norms, the question of the validity of that highest-level norm still arises. Put otherwise, we might be able to identify or dream up a number of systems of rules, with their own internal structure and organizing highest norms. The question we would need to answer is which of those systems is in force as the legal system of a particular place. The challenge for the positivist, then, is to tell us what matter of fact establishes that a particular system of legal norms is in force.

For Bentham and Austin, the solution lay in a certain account of sovereignty. Law, "strictly and properly so-called" as Austin liked to put it, was the command of a sovereign, backed up with a threatened sanction. This position is positivist because commands can be identified as events that happen in the world, and the sovereign, the person or collective whose commands count as law, is also identified purely descriptively. The sovereign is not such because of some right to rule, but because of the existence of a habit of obedience. Therefore, to find out the content of the law it is necessary to figure out whose commands are habitually obeyed and then figure out what he has commanded.

Hart's detailed criticism of the command theory has been very influential (though for some reasonable doubts, see Schauer 2010a). Part of the critique pointed out that many legal rules are only very awkwardly understood as commands. The rules of contract law, for example, are better understood as facilitative than imperative. Also, the idea that all legal rules are backed with sanctions cannot be made to fit much of what is commonly regarded as law. (For example, Austin had to concede that, according to his view, a statute repealing another statute was not strictly a law.)

Hart's alternative account is that the validity of legal rules is determined by other legal rules in a hierarchical structure that ends with a set of ultimate criteria of legal validity, identified as such by a rule called the rule of recognition. But this special rule is not really a rule *of* the system of legal sources; rather it is a rule definitive of the system, grounding it from outside. To avoid the question, "But how do we know that the rule of recognition is valid?" Hart holds that it is neither valid nor invalid, it just is. By which he means, it is the rule of recognition that is *in effect*. It is the rule of recognition that the participants in the practice of making, but especially applying, the law in a particular place actually *accept* – they treat it as appropriately governing their activities within the legal practice. The situation is analogous to the "rule" that tells us that the rules of chess are the rules of chess. How do we know that *these* are the rules of the game, rather than *those*? No rule of the game of chess can answer that question. We can only answer, well, these are the rules that are generally accepted to be the rules of chess.

It seems evident to most commentators that Hart's account of law is superior to Austin's. Given that there is so much disagreement about the nature of law, this area of agreement might seem puzzling. We cannot say that it seems evident to everyone that Hart has more accurately described the nature of law, because it does not seem so to nonpositivists – from their point of view, both accounts are utterly hopeless. The best way to characterize the relationship between the command theory and Hart's account is that they are competing efforts to provide detail for the basic picture of law as social fact. If that basic picture is taken for granted, Hart's account is better to the extent that it fits better with our ordinary contemporary ways of talking and thinking about the law. The great achievement of *The Concept of Law* is to tell a story about how the law is determined purely by social facts that appears entirely natural, even commonsensical, to the reader who is already attracted by that basic picture.

There is superficially a great contrast here with the work of Hans Kelsen.[2] Kelsen's commitment to a "presupposed" valid *Grundnorm* ("basic norm") as the final step on the ladder of validity strikes many people, at least in the English-speaking world, as philosophically extravagant and obtuse. But actually the difference between Hart's and Kelsen's accounts is not nearly as great as it may seem, and for a rather banal reason: Though both wrote that they were giving accounts of legal "validity" ("*Geltung*"), they meant different things by the word (Raz 1979, 150). For Hart, the ultimate criteria of validity as set out in a rule of recognition simply identify those rules that are "in force," or are part of the law, in a particular place. This leaves open, as an issue requiring separate discussion, what reason, if any, a person might have to obey those rules. In his rejection of Austin's account of law, Hart pointed out that for many people legal rules play a significant deliberative role; they are not simply

---

[2] Kelsen's views changed over time. My account, which is heavily influenced by Raz 1979, is based mainly on Kelsen 1967, but seems compatible with earlier and later publications. For discussion of the development of Kelsen's views, see Paulson 1998.

obeyed out of habit, but are treated as providing reasons for action. He also introduced the idea of "internal" legal statements – those that, in making claims about the law that is in force, express the utterer's acceptance of the legal norms as reason giving. For example, the statement, "it is my legal duty to pay my taxes," is, for Hart, an internal legal statement in this sense. But all of this is compatible with the possibility that valid legal rules provide no one with any genuine reason for action at all; in particular, neither the fact that a rule is legally valid nor people's willingness to make internal statements about that rule implies anything about its moral force. Hart did believe that he had to provide an account of the discourse of "legal obligation," but that account too leaves quite open the issue of whether I have a real reason to do what I have a legal obligation to do. Law, in this sense, is just like the system of rules we call etiquette, or indeed any rule-governed game; we can make sense of proper and improper moves we can make from within the game, without taking any kind of stand about why that is a game we should play. This aspect of Hart's view is discussed further in Chapter 7.

Kelsen used the term "validity" differently. For Kelsen, legal norms purport to impose oughts, and insofar as they are valid, they do impose oughts. There is some controversy about whether Kelsen thought that legal oughts were in some sense a different kind of beast than moral oughts, but such a distinction would only matter for current purposes if he also thought that legal oughts were somehow less binding than moral oughts, which he clearly did not. And so the reason Kelsen had to insist that the foundation of a legal system was a presupposed basic *norm* rather than some matter of fact, was that, as he saw it, validity implies ought and you can't get an ought from an is. As Kelsen (1928, 393–4) puts it, "This, indeed, is the problem of the positivity of law: The law appears as 'ought' and 'is' at the same time, while logically these two categories are mutually exclusive."

Nonetheless, facts are the foundation of the grounds of law for Kelsen as well. The content of law for Kelsen is determined by the rules of the constitution that is effective, and a constitution is effective if the norms created in accordance with it are by and large applied and obeyed. It is just that those norms are only legally *valid* in Kelsen's sense if there is a further norm, the basic norm, which states that people ought to obey the effective constitution. Without that grounding ought statement, there would only be matters of fact, no oughts. That would do for a sociological account of law, but not for a "juristic" one (Kelsen 1967, 218).

So we see that both Hart and Kelsen offer accounts of how to determine which legal norms are in force without at the same time taking a stand on whether they impose genuine obligations. Hart calls this an account of legal validity, while Kelsen insists that it is not yet that. There is no need to quibble over these words. I generally use "validity" in Hart's normatively neutral sense because it seems to comport with current English usage. The issue of what kind of obligation valid legal rules can impose is discussed in Chapter 7, and that is the right place to discuss Kelsen's doctrine of the basic norm (see also Marmor 2010).

The question we are addressing now is how to determine the content of the law that is in force. And though Hart's account of the law that is in force is in some ways an advance on Kelsen's, it is fundamentally the same view. For Hart, the content of the law is determined by the ultimate criteria of legal validity. The ultimate criteria of legal validity are set out in the rule of recognition, which is in effect if it is actually followed by people in the business of identifying law. The content of law for Kelsen is determined by the rules of the constitution that is effective. The "constitution," in this usage, means the collection of rules regulating the creation of legal norms that apply to people, and is in that sense roughly equivalent to Hart's rule of recognition, which sets out ultimate criteria of legal validity (Kelsen 2006, 124; 1967, 222). A constitution is effective if the norms created in accordance with it are by and large applied and obeyed. On both accounts, then, law has the content it does because of certain facts about the practice of people, especially legal officials.[3]

---

[3] Hart believes that unless officials take an "internal attitude" to the rule of recognition, a legal system will not persist. But this internal attitude is still a matter of fact. Whether

It might seem that on these accounts of how to determine the law in force we have not just given up on Kelsen's thought that to say a legal norm is valid is to say that it is genuinely binding; we have also given up on any plausible understanding of the law as a set of norms at all. For whether or not it imposes genuine obligations, it must be possible, if law is to be understood as a set of norms, for there to be divergence between what the law requires and what happens in legal practice; that seems hard to square with the idea that the content of the law is determined by matters of fact. But the positivist model of how to determine the content of law – not just the model of Hart and Kelsen, but also that of Bentham and Austin – is compatible with this minimal sense in which law is a set of norms. It does not reject the idea that there is a truth of the matter about what the law is in particular places and that legal officials can be mistaken about this. On the command model, a judge could go wrong in misunderstanding the content of the sovereign's command. In Hart and Kelsen's version, a decision might be mistaken when a particular legal official decides contrary to the constitutional norms that are generally applied, or simply fails to reason correctly within the normative system the ultimate criteria of validity set up.

To sum up: the positivist picture of law is distinctive in finding the grounds of the law, the ultimate sources of its content, in matters of fact. Reducing the accounts of Hart and Kelsen to what is relevant to an account of the grounds of law (as opposed to an account of the role law plays in the deliberations of most legal officials, or an account of what kind of obligation, if any, law imposes), we extract a plausible way to fill out this picture: the social facts that provide the grounds for the content of law are practices that most legal officials actually engage in most of the time. In saying that it is plausible, I mean that for those of us who find the picture of law as social fact appealing in the first place, this account introduces no awkwardness; it is compatible with us (including those of

officials can in fact treat the rule of recognition as providing reasons for action is discussed further in the next section.

us who live in constitutional democracies) continuing to say most of the things we are in the habit of saying about the law.

Positivist Puzzles

If we take Hart's formulations as our positivist model, there are some ambiguities to unravel and revisions to be made. Hart (1994, 110) writes: "The rule of recognition exists only as a complex, but normally concordant, practice of the courts, officials, and private persons in identifying the law by reference to certain criteria. Its existence is a matter of fact." It is this formulation that is closest to Kelsen's account of the efficacy of a constitution.

Hart also tells us that the officials of a legal system must *accept* the rule of recognition. On the notion of acceptance introduced to illustrate the idea of the internal point of view, those who accept a rule treat it as providing a general reason for action that also applies to others and justifies criticism, of themselves and the others, for noncompliance. Just why they treat the rule in this way is, as we have seen, entirely open. It could be because they believe that prudence counsels it, or morality demands it, or because, like most other people, they just do, without having thought much about it.

The rule of recognition, Hart tells us,

> if it is to exist at all, must be regarded from the internal point of view as a public, common standard of correct judicial decision, and not as something which each judge merely obeys for his part only. Individual courts of the system though they may, on occasion, deviate from these rules must, in general, be critically concerned with such deviations as lapses from standards, which are essentially common or public. This is not merely a matter of the efficiency or health of the legal system, but is logically a necessary condition of our ability to speak of the existence of a single system.

The unity and continuity of the legal system, he goes on, "depends on the acceptance, at this crucial point, of common standards of legal validity" (116).

But if "acceptance" here means what it usually does – treating the rule as a reason for action – this is puzzling, since "common standards of legal validity" cannot provide, all on their own, a reason for action.

In Hart's model of law as the union of primary and secondary rules, the former are "duty-imposing" and the latter "power-conferring."[4] There is a sense in which both kinds of rule can guide action. Hart's secondary rules of adjudication and change specify how legal disputes are to be authoritatively resolved and how law is changed in the system. These rules tell people what official role they need to attain and what they need to do if they are, in accordance with law, to resolve a particular dispute according to law or to change the law. Similarly, the rule of recognition tells someone wishing to declare the content of law how to do that. But these rules guide action hypothetically – "if you want to do that, this is the way to do it" – just like a recipe or the rules of a game. None of them provides categorical reasons – "do this!" – for action. Hart's rule of adjudication should not be confused with a theory of adjudication as discussed in the previous chapter, that directs those with the official role of deciding legal disputes how that should be done; it is rather a rule that tells us who has the authority to decide disputes and according to what formal processes (97). The rule of change similarly tells us which kinds of acts of which people or assemblies will be effective in making law, not that anyone should make law.

Our interest is in the rule of recognition. People can of course accept that they should comply with or apply the law, and if they do they will need to know the content of the rule of recognition. But in accepting a norm – treating it as a reason for action – that I should comply with or apply law as identified by the rule of recognition, I am not accepting the "common standards of legal validity." I cannot treat a rule that simply specifies the ultimate criteria of legal validity as itself a reason for

---

[4] Some power-conferring rules, such as rules of contract law, are not secondary rules according to another way of marking the distinction that Hart sometimes employs – according to which secondary rules are rules about other rules. The infelicities of Hart's distinction have been much discussed, but I won't explore them here.

action. I treat the norm "feed your children nutritious food" as a reason for action, but I cannot treat principles of good nutrition themselves as reasons for action.[5]

The whole thing makes much more sense if we regard the rule of recognition as no practical rule at all, but rather a simple statement of ultimate criteria that one may hold correct or not. From this perspective, we can read Hart's use of the word "acceptance" when discussing the rule of recognition as meaning something other than it usually does for him. We can say that the officials must accept that these are the actual ultimate criteria of validity for this legal system in the sense that they must believe that they are, or be disposed to treat them as such. It *would* be a problem if no one actually thought that the criteria of validity they appealed to in any particular instance were the real ultimate criteria of validity, applicable alike to all cases concerning all people. It is plausible to say that for a legal system to continue and have unity the officials of the system, those who have de facto power and administer it in the name of law, must converge in what they regard the ultimate criteria of validity within the system to be. If each official believed that the criteria applied "for their part only" we would, as Hart writes, "be in the presence of a *lusus naturae* worth thinking about only because it sharpens our awareness of what is often too obvious to be noticed" (116). So the matter of external fact that determines whether a rule of recognition "exists" is, we

---

[5] Raz (1979, 92–3) interprets Hart as holding that the rule of recognition is not just a statement of common standards of legal validity, but a duty-imposing rule, imposing duties on law-applying officials. See also Coleman 2001a, 84–6. I argued in the previous chapter that judges can in principle fully discharge their official obligations without developing a view about the content of the law already in force; so in principle, positivist judges do not need to know what the rule of recognition is. But supposing that judges have a legal duty to figure out what the law is, the interpretation makes sense. But now do legal officials, as a matter of "logic," need to accept, in the "treat as reason-giving" sense, that they must either comply with or apply law, either as subjects of officials? It doesn't seem that the existence of a legal system depends on this, though certainly its health and efficiency would. What matters is that legal officials do comply with or apply the law, not why. If case-by-case self-interest were sufficient to ensure compliance by officials, that would be enough. See further Chapters 7 and 8.

should say, convergence in belief or attitude among legal officials about the ultimate criteria of validity.

Is this interpretation compatible with Hart's statement that the rule of recognition exists as a practice of the "law-identifying and law-enforcing agencies effective in a given territory"? (Hart 1984, 336; see also Raz 1979, 90–7; 1999, 132–48). Let us use Raz's useful label "law-applying institutions" to cover both kinds of institution and understand Hart's "legal officials" as the people who staff them. The question is: What exactly is the "practice" by these officials that is supposed to reveal the content of the rule of recognition? As we have seen in the previous chapter, looking at what courts and other legal decision makers actually do and say will reveal (if we assume that all these decision makers are conscientious) implicit theories of adjudication, but not necessarily beliefs about criteria of legal validity.

The same clearly goes for law-enforcing agencies. The conscientious police officer will, we hope, believe that law sets limits to what she can do in her official capacity; but no one would think that her beliefs about the law could be read off from what she does. Kelsen's (1967, 349) image of the law providing a frame only, leaving particular determinations to the law applier's discretion, is uncontroversial when applied to law enforcers.

Hart's view that the primary source of information about the grounds of law was the practice of legal officials is appealing because it suggests a close connection between de facto political power and the content of effective law. It also promises to allow us to say that law is grounded in very concrete social facts – facts about what people do and say. But it turns out that these two positivist desires cannot be satisfied together.

The only *practice* that would directly and reliably reveal beliefs about ultimate criteria of legal validity is that of legal experts, particularly legal academics, in preparing textbooks and other presentations of the state of current law. This would reduce positivism to the unhappy view that the ultimate criteria of legal validity are found in a rule that exists as a practice of law professors.

The better solution is simply to abandon the idea that the rule of recognition exists as a social practice in any straightforward sense. The rule of recognition, if it exists, is a set of common beliefs and or attitudes, perhaps implicit, about the ultimate grounds of law and/or dispositions about what to regard or treat as the ultimate criteria when figuring out what the law is.

When we now consider whose beliefs count, Hart's association of the foundations of law with legal officialdom is largely but not wholly vindicated. Most people who do not work with the law have only vague and uncertain beliefs about ultimate criteria of legal validity. Among officials, some have more comprehensive interaction with law than others, and it is natural to think that the more comprehensively a person is involved with the law, the more that person's beliefs count in fixing the grounds of law. So Hart's frequent emphasis on the courts is justified; but the beliefs of legal officials in, for example, law departments of the executive branch should be regarded as especially significant also.

However, though officials are clearly the central case, it would be more accurate to say that we are looking, more generally, for convergence in belief about the ultimate criteria among those who work with the law in their professional capacities. This expands the net beyond officials of the state to include practicing lawyers and academic legal experts. The intuition here is that even if all state officials started, for example, to declare that some formerly embraced constitutional principle was not a source of law, we would not immediately be inclined to say that the rule of recognition had changed if all lawyers and legal experts disagreed. At the limit, too, it is wholly possible for an entire population to have beliefs about the ultimate criteria of validity, and if its beliefs were sufficiently comprehensive and convergent, that would be relevant to the issue of what the law is should some officials start to head off in a different direction (Adler 2006; Tamanaha 2001, 166–7).

Now the appeal to convergence in belief about criteria of validity among those with a life in the law may seem hopelessly optimistic. Dworkin has always denied that any such convergence exists, even among judges. One response from positivists has been to point out that there is an important difference between agreement on the proper standards for determining legal validity and agreement on the correct application of those standards in a particular case (Coleman 2001a, 116). This is certainly true; the positivist need not be embarrassed just by the fact that two people might apply the same legal rule to the same facts and arrive at different conclusions. This is as true for standards of legal validity as for primary legal rules that apply directly to people. Two people may agree entirely on a criterion for the legal enforceability of agreements (there must be a mutuality of interest in the exchange, say), but disagree about whether a particular agreement is enforceable; and there could be consensus that statutes that have not been enforced for a very long time are no longer valid but much disagreement about how long, in this context, is long enough.

This point can only take us so far, however. Even if all acknowledge the same text as setting out ultimate criteria of validity, disagreement about the proper method of interpretation of that text can undermine consensus about the grounds of law. One group might hold, for example, that a certain eighteenth-century text should be read with an eye to what would best advance some purpose (perhaps not stated in the text) in the contemporary world, while another might hold that it must be understood to mean what a literal-minded eighteenth-century reader would have thought it meant. When we say that there is agreement about the grounds of law, we must mean more than that all recognize certain canonical statements of criteria of validity to be correct. "Manifestly unreasonable legislation is invalid" for example, is clearly of no use as a criterion of validity unless we have some ideas about the relevant notion of reasonableness.

If there is to be a rule of recognition, there must be genuine consensus about the ultimate criteria of legal validity, not nominal consensus that consists in a general willingness to use the same form of words.[6] Of

---

[6] I believe this is the fundamental insight of "The Model of Rules I" (Dworkin 1978, 14–45).

course, a rule of recognition can have gaps – there may be no consensus on some questions of validity even if there is consensus on many. It is an open and complicated question how much agreement of the right kind there is in any particular place. But I will postpone further discussion of this issue until Chapter 6, where the problem of disagreement will be taken to the next level, the level of disagreement about the nature of law itself.

For now, there are other positivist puzzles to consider. On the positivist account, the foundations of law lie in people's beliefs and attitudes about the foundations of law. Many people have nonpositivist views about law; they may believe that the ultimate criteria are determined, in the end, by some argument having to do with the legitimacy of the state. For example, they may believe that a constitution sets out the ultimate criteria of legal validity just because the scheme of government it sets up constitutes a legitimate coercive political order. Our positivist does not have any difficulty with the fact that some beliefs about ultimate criteria are based on what (to the positivist) are mistaken views about law. All the positivist looks at is what the beliefs about the grounds of law are, not the justification someone might offer for those beliefs. What is interesting is that it is much harder to make sense of the beliefs of the positivists among us.

If we are positivists, we think that the grounds of law are what we think the grounds of law are. It can seem that there is nothing else for us to be thinking about, when we are thinking about the grounds of law, other than what we think.

We do have ideas about what legal norms are. At the least, we think legal norms are directives that present themselves as legitimate demands on our conduct. Those who create those norms, those whose institutional role it is to pronounce their application to particular cases, and those whose institutional role it is to enforce them, all present their institutional acts as justified. As discussed further in later chapters, this seems to be the truth in Raz's important idea that law claims authority. Something like these ideas must be in our minds as we distinguish legal norms from norms of morality, conventional morality, etiquette, or the rules of a game.[7] But for the positivist, these ideas themselves do not give us any basis on which to identify the grounds of law. When it comes to that, all we have to go on is our beliefs about the grounds of law, and those beliefs are themselves not justified by any further set of considerations. The puzzle is that when it comes to the question of what the ultimate criteria are for determining the content of law, there is nothing substantive for each of us to be thinking *about*.

Some have suggested that the rule of recognition is best seen as the conventional solution to a coordination problem. A coordination problem is one where the substance of the solution is not what matters (whether we drive on the left or on the right), but the fact that we all agree on what it is. If this were a plausible way to think about law, it might make sense of the puzzle. If law is just a conventional solution to a coordination problem, it is not surprising that there is no substantive basis to anyone's view about the grounds of law, since it wouldn't matter what the grounds of law were, just so long as there were some.

But of course this isn't how we think about law (Dickson 2007; Green 1999). We think it matters a lot whether the king's command, or the court's opinion, or the acts of parliament are sources of law. This is what makes natural Dworkin's claim that beliefs about the grounds of law really are, in the end, grounded in political theory. On Dworkin's view, there is something for each of us to think about when we reflect on the foundations of law; we are to think about what might make the resulting government by law legitimate and potentially just. The positivist agrees that that's what we should think about when we are thinking about what the grounds of law should be, but denies its relevance when we are thinking about what they are.

The solution to the puzzle of what each positivist is supposed to think about, when asked what he believes are the ultimate criteria of validity, is

---

[7] In Chapter 8, I discuss further what we might have in mind when we are thinking about a norm as legal, rather than something else.

found in the history of law.[8] In an ongoing legal system, judges, law professors, and so on are not reduced to asking each other what they think at any particular time. One thing they all believe, for a variety of reasons, is that the ultimate criteria of legal validity do not typically change radically from moment to moment. And so there is something to anchor all our beliefs about the grounds of law now; it is what we know about what has been generally believed up until now. There is, in this respect, an important historicist aspect to positivism, whether it be based on the command theory (habits of obedience build up only over time) or the model of the system of norms.

But of course legal orders can undergo revolutionary change. When change happens, the relevant people can no longer look to history to ground their beliefs about criteria of legal validity, and so a different account is needed. The positivist account of radical constitutional change must be that relevant people somehow reach the position, at roughly the same time, that it would be better if *these* were the ultimate criteria of validity (those set out in the new constitution) rather than *those* (the constitutional rules that had been traditionally followed). People's reasons for thinking that these criteria would be better than those may or may not be grounded in moral beliefs; they may also be grounded in a convergence in people's sense of their own interests. But again, what matters is not why they believe this, but that they become disposed to identify law with reference to the new criteria.

The success of this kind of revolutionary legal reform depends on everyone connected with law going along with it. If from one day to the next, these people start treating different factors as determinative of legal validity, then the revolution has succeeded. When it comes to fundamental constitutional change, as Hart memorably put it, "all that succeeds is success" (1994, 153). It should be noted, however, that the expanded account of whose beliefs count for determining the existence of the rule of recognition offered earlier forces some changes to Hart's

---

[8] I am heavily influenced here and in what follows by Marmor 2009, 155–75.

account of fundamental constitutional change. On that account, if all the legal officials embrace a new rule of recognition, then the rule of recognition will have changed. But on the broader account I have argued is necessary, the legal officials would have to bring everyone else with a life in the law along with them. And this is intuitively right – a fact that supports the broader view. For if the officials embrace one set of criteria while all the nonofficial lawyers and legal experts reject it, we would be more inclined to talk in terms of an illegal coup d'état, as opposed to a successful legal change.

At the moment of revolution, when relevant people become disposed to identify law by reference to the new criteria, it would be misleading to say that there was a convergence of *belief* about ultimate legal criteria. Deciding to treat certain factors as the grounds of law is not the same as believing that they are the grounds of law. But this is not embarrassing for the positivist story. The situation is closely analogous to inventing rules for a new game, or drastically changing the rules for a game with an existing name. Andrei Marmor's (2009) notion of a constitutive convention is helpful here. We can say that, at the moment of revolution, the members of the relevant group are disposed to appeal to certain criteria to determine legal validity, contingent on their belief that others are similarly disposed. The reasons people have for being disposed to appeal to a particular set of criteria are not *just* that they believe others will – they have substantive reasons, good or bad, for hoping that others will. But, as positivists, they will not, at the revolutionary moment, appeal to those criteria unless they expect others to, because they believe that consensus on the relevant criteria is required before the new legal order can take effect. If all goes well for the revolutionaries, there will be a convergence and a new legal order will have been constituted. Once people believe that this has happened, then they can straightforwardly be said to have beliefs about the grounds of law. And from that moment onward, there is no need to think about the rule of recognition as a convention in any strong sense that implies that part of the reason people have for thinking that such and such are the ultimate criteria is that everyone else does as well.

The situation here is exactly analogous to the emergence of a new norm of customary international law. A rule of customary international law exists when there is a general practice of states attended by an "opinio juris" – the belief that the practice is a case of following the law. There is an apparent paradox, or circle, in this criterion; it appears that belief that the practice is legally required has to precede its being legally required – which, unless law is to be founded on irrational or false beliefs, seems impossible. It would be irrational to come to believe, for no reason at all, that a practice until now not legally required is legally required. The solution is the same as that just sketched for change in the rule of recognition.

First, there is no problem with rules of long standing. Everyone relevant may believe that such and such is a customary rule of law just because that's what has generally been believed for a long time. There is nothing irrational or puzzling about that (Tasioulas 2007, 322). As with the rule of recognition, the problem comes with changes in customary international law. It would be rational to come to believe that a practice is legally required on the basis of a reasonable but false belief that there is a general belief that it is legally required, but it would be troubling if this were the only way a new customary norm could get off the ground. But there is a non-troubling possibility, which we might call the orthodox route to a practice becoming legally required. States may converge in the belief that it would be good if a certain practice had the status of law, and so be disposed to treat it as law so long as enough others do. Once the initial leap is made, and enough others are treating the practice as law, the belief of any one state that the practice is law need not be contingent on everyone else's attitudes or dispositions anymore and the validity of the rule will just depend on the fact that most states believe it is law.[9]

---

[9] I return to customary international law in Chapter 8. The literature on the so-called chronological paradox is voluminous; I find Lefkowitz 2008 especially helpful.

Inclusive and Exclusive

The fact that fixes the grounds of law on the positivist account I have outlined is a convergence of beliefs or dispositions among those with a life in
the law. But now there is an apparent problem linking this view with the
main feature of the picture of law as fact as I have outlined it – the idea
that it is never necessary to appeal to moral considerations to determine
what the law is. For of course many people do believe that moral considerations are relevant to the determination of legal validity.

On the one hand there is the firm conviction, best expressed in the
works of Raz, that law is found in a morally neutral interpretation of
valid legal materials. On the other hand, there is the basic positivist
position that the validity of legal materials is determined by contingencies of the beliefs or practices of legal officials and relevant others. The problem is that, at the top of the ladder of positivist validity,
beliefs about the ultimate criteria of legal validity might not be consistent with the idea that morality is never relevant to determining the
content of law.

Positivism splits at this point. If you focus on the motivation for
being a positivist in the first place – the desire to be able to insist that
the content of the law is one thing, its moral merit another – the exclusivist position is irresistible. In Raz's (1994) terminology, the exclusivist
view is that the grounds of law are all socially identified *sources* that can
be interpreted without recourse to moral judgment. If we take this view
about the nature of law, moral standards simply cannot be part of law.
So moral language in legal materials will be read not as part of law but
as directing a decision maker to make a judgment, outside the bounds
of law, on the moral merits. If legal officials and the rest believe that, to
the contrary, those moral-sounding requirements in the materials really
are cases where morality is incorporated into law, that belief must simply be ignored. A belief that some unwritten overarching moral standard
of validity is among the ultimate criteria must likewise be ignored. On
the exclusive positivist account, we determine the grounds of law by

appeal to a purification of a consensus among relevant people about the grounds of law.

There is nothing objectionable about this way of proceeding. The main positivist idea that law is grounded in fact is not itself justified by asserting that everyone believes this. Rather, philosophical argument is required to get us to that point. The exclusive position is that law is grounded in social sources, read straight, and that the beliefs of those with lives in the law about what the social sources are settles the matter.

The inclusive position is that law is grounded in social sources along with moral considerations that those with a life in the law agree are relevant. In other words, the content of the rule of recognition itself will determine whether grossly unjust rules or standards can be valid, whether a "moral reading" of sources is always appropriate, or whether "moral language" in sources incorporates just those aspects of morality into law.[10]

On each view, certain beliefs of legal participants become relevant once a certain account of the grounds of law is accepted (that law is grounded in facts about beliefs and attitudes of those with a life in the law). On each view, certain beliefs about the grounds of law held by legal participants must simply be ignored – for example, that there can be no law that contravenes God's will. But the views differ on whether beliefs that certain moral considerations are among the rounds of law must be ignored. How to choose between these views?

Both versions of positivism are perfectly coherent. The exclusive view seems overwhelmingly more appealing to someone with an initial picture of law as fact; but then the inclusive view sits more comfortably when we are discussing some aspects of legal practice. I will not here address the

---

[10] I leave aside a view that holds that where "moral language" is found in a source, there morality is incorporated into law by that very fact, irrespective of the content of the rule of recognition. The problem with this view, as Raz (2004) has discussed, is that some argument is required, from within the positivist outlook, for assuming that the moral considerations a judge is, the externalist agrees, thereby directed to consider when making a decision, are themselves part of law.

internecine arguments between these two positions, since, as I argue in Chapter 6, we lack compelling argument at the more basic level: we lack compelling argument for preferring either version of positivism to any version of nonpositivism.[11]

I will, however, make one remark, without further comment, about the internal debate: the inclusive position seems reactive, driven by the need to reply to various objections to positivism. The exclusive position, by contrast, is motivated by a strong sense of law's validity being entirely distinct from its goodness. If no one had this initial conviction about the nature of law, I doubt that the very idea of positivism would ever have emerged. The nonpositivist position is driven by the opposite conviction that law occupies the same general space as the good and the required; that's just the kind of thing law is. It seems to me that no primitive pre-theoretical motivation for the inclusive positivist position exists. It stakes out a middle ground that makes positivism seem less jarring when considering, in particular, constitutional adjudication grounded on bills of rights (Waluchow 1994). But this middle ground seems unstable, since once we have become comfortable with the idea that the content of law is sometimes fixed by the truth about what is good and right, it isn't so clear why we have reason to resist the nonpositivist view that considerations of the good and the right are always relevant to the content of law. In other words, in the positivist conviction that law is a matter of fact, not morality, it is the second, negative part of that thought that seems to me dominant.

---

[11] Inclusive legal positive is defended in Coleman 2001a and Waluchow 1994; Himma 2002 is a helpful shorter discussion.

4 Nonpositivism

Good Things about Law

Most people who take any kind of interest in the debate about the nature of law seem to have very strong views, right from the start. Either positivism or nonpositivism is obviously right and the other obviously wrong. What seems obviously wrong about positivism to many is that it misses the fact that law in its nature is something good, or can be seen as striving toward being something good – or at the very least, is something that can't be very bad. For most people of this inclination, the evident truth that law is something good, or at least potentially so, is tied up with the further evident truth that the law is genuinely binding on us, or is usually so, or is in some sense *meant* to be so (Greenberg 2011) – it is, as Dworkin all along insisted, a domain of *real* rights and obligations. To see law as ultimately grounded in social fact is to miss these essential moral qualities of law. From this point of view, it may turn out that the Nazis and the Taliban have no law, but who cares about that? If something interesting is going on in this whole domain, something worth reflecting on, especially something worth reflecting on philosophically, it must be because there is something valuable or at least potentially valuable about law, or at any rate something immediately morally relevant about law, and part of the philosophical task is to figure out what that is (see, for example, Perry 2001, Soper 1984).

To be clear about the contrast here, we have to remember that positivists of course agree that there is something potentially valuable about law.

45

Good law is good. They may even agree that, wherever there is law, there you are likely, or even certain, to find something that is in one way good – an effective legal system will greatly increase the range of social possibilities, and we may say that this, in itself, is in one way good. They also are likely to say that, depending on the law's content, there are often moral obligations to obey (some of) it. As we will see in Chapter 7, it is consistent with positivism to believe that especially certain kinds of law (those that apply to states) are very likely to generate reasons for action. The disagreement is that the nonpositivist insists that the inherent moral significance of law must be kept in mind when thinking about what kind of thing law is, and, in turn, must structure any theory of how to determine legal content in any particular place. The positivist, by contrast, believes that we can account for law's nature while bracketing any moral significance it may have. I argue in Chapters 6 and 7 that the fact that law can have moral significance should be the reason that anyone engages in the exercise of providing a theory of the grounds of law in the first place. But for the positivist, that theory itself is not shaped by any view about law's value.

That we are describing something of inherent moral significance is a common assumption of nonpositivism, but this broad idea could be explicated in many different ways. Since the late 1960s, nonpositivism has rightly come to be associated with Dworkin's legal theory. This theory is both deep and complex, and it contains many strong commitments that it is worthwhile to identify individually, so that we can better see the range of nonpositivist options.

Morality in the Grounds of Law: The Moral Reading and the Moral Filter

What I take to be definitional of all nonpositivist views is that moral considerations are always among the grounds of law. Morality can figure in determining law's content in two main ways. In the first, it is always playing a role as a guide to interpretation, resolving indeterminacy and perhaps also correcting particular mistakes in the law to show the law as a whole in its morally best light. This view has its roots in common-law legal theory and was developed into a comprehensive theory of legal interpretation by Dworkin. The term "interpretivism" is sometimes (Dworkin 2011, 401; Stavropoulos, 2003) used as a label for Dworkin's view, but since any theory of law acknowledges that legal materials require interpretation, I prefer a more revealing label that Dworkin (1996) also used – "the moral reading." As one common formulation of this approach has it, the law is what follows from the principles that best justify past legal practice.

A different kind of nonpositivism takes a blunter approach. As is well known to English-speaking legal theorists thanks to discussion in Hart's (1958) article "Positivism and the Separation of Law and Morals," Gustav Radbruch came to the conclusion that a positivist view of law was partly to blame for the degree of obedience to Nazi law the German population displayed during the Third Reich. In response, Radbruch developed the idea that it was contrary to the nature of law that it could, in its content, be seriously unjust. Thus much of what was presented as law by the Nazi regime was not law at all. As noted in Chapter 2, at least one German court embraced the so-called Radbruch formula in another reconstruction era – the reunification of Germany after the fall of the Berlin Wall in the late twentieth century.

The view that nothing can be law that is very unjust is essentially (some form of) positivism, with a moral filter laid on top. The thought here is that, even though law isn't always perfect, we rebel at the thought of what might be called perversions of law. An institutionalized system of rules and standards that avowedly is aimed at genocide cannot, on this view, fall within the domain of law. The most prominent defender of the moral filter view at the turn of the twenty-first century is Robert Alexy; his argument for the moral filter is discussed briefly in Chapter 6.

Legality, Legitimacy, and Justice

Both the moral reading and the moral filter need to be further specified, as perhaps not just any moral consideration is relevant to the interpretation of law. One might hold, for example, that what is good about law is that it regulates social life in a way that respects the autonomy of its members and treats them all as equals before the law.

That some version of the ideal of the rule of law shapes our understanding of the nature of law was the view of Lon Fuller (1969). Fuller's main line of argument is that unless the entire legal system satisfies certain formal criteria, none of the rules or standards within it can count as law. This view is discussed further in Chapter 8, where we will evaluate, in the context of a discussion of international law, various views about the necessary features of legal systems. But Fuller also thought that considerations of the rule of law, or legality, should shape legal interpretation (Rundle 2012, 168–74). Without trying to do justice to the complexity of Fuller's actual position, his writings do suggest this view about how to figure out what the law is: when interpreting legal materials, one must do so with an eye to making them consistent with the ideal of the rule of law. This is in fact how Dworkin describes his moral reading, but his account of the rule of law is expansive enough to encompass all moral considerations necessary to reach a conclusion about the proper resolution of a particular dispute (see, for example, Dworkin 2006, 170).

For there to be a distinctive view here, rule-of-law values must be thought to make up a subset of potentially morally relevant factors – a distinctly *legal* morality as Fuller conceived it. This would exclude, for example, the liberal theory of social justice that is among the resources of Dworkin's moral reading. The richest defense of such a view can be found in the work of David Dyzenhaus (2000, 2007). On such a restricted moral reading, it would seem that preexisting law would not always be sufficiently determinate to resolve a particular dispute. Reading legal materials in light of classical rule-of-law values such as publicity, prospectivity, and equality before the law would clearly reduce indeterminacy as compared to a positivist nonmoral reading, but it is hard to see that this limited set of moral considerations would be sufficient to allow us to say that existing law provides an answer to all legal disputes. Dworkin's more expansive understanding of the values encompassed by the rule of law seems necessary for him to make good on his well-known claim that the law always already provides a "right answer."[1]

As discussed in the next chapter, the content of the ideal of the rule of law is just as contested as the nature of law. It is therefore not helpful to sort nonpositivist views according to whether they hold that the grounds of law include the values of the rule of law or more than that. The point is simply that within both the moral filter and moral reading approaches, a range of options exists about what kinds of moral considerations are appropriately appealed to in legal interpretation. It seems on the face of things that just as exclusive positivism best expresses the initial foundational belief that law is about what is and not about what ought to be or what is good, a maximalist nonpositivist view such as Dworkin's best expresses the initial foundational belief that law is a domain of value. On the other hand, as Dyzenhaus (2000, 2007) explains, there are advantages to the restricted moral reading, in that the moral considerations held to be among the grounds of law emerge from the very idea of legal governance, rather than a contestable moral and political theory. I will not here attempt an internal evaluation of these options for nonpositivists.

It does seem, however, that the moral reading is straightforwardly more plausible than the moral filter, since once we believe that the content of law is partly determined by moral considerations, it seems unmotivated to recognize a discontinuity, such that morality is involved only when the law would otherwise be very bad. After all, the moral reading, as a reading of legal materials, preserves the institutional positivity of law; it does not go all the way to the position that legal norms just are morally ideal norms.

---

[1] Jeremy Waldron's (2008) argument that the grounds of law include rule-of-law values characterizes those values as ones of procedure and form. There are, however, signs that Waldron is ready to embrace an account of legality as expansive as Dworkin's. He writes that when judges disagree about how to resolve hard cases – when there is no disagreement about the terms of any relevant statute or precedent – judges are disagreeing about what the law (already) is, by way of disagreeing about the content of the ideal of the rule of law (48–54). This suggests that any moral factor relevant to figuring out how to resolve the dispute is a rule-of-law value.

Justification and Obligation

Among those who approach the theory of law from the nonpositivist foundational stance, some, such as Dworkin, assert the strong claim that legal rights and duties are always real, that is moral, rights and duties. The topic of the normativity of law is discussed in Chapter 7. For now, the important point is that if we hold as a fixed point that legal rights and duties are moral rights and duties, the moral reasoning in legal interpretation may take on a distinctive structure. Whether it will do so will depend on our moral theory of the duty to obey the law, however. Thus if we believe that legal rights and duties are real rights and duties just because we believe that all subjects have, in a relevant sense, consented or promised to obey, legal interpretation will not be affected. If, however, we hold, with Dworkin, that legal rights and duties are moral rights and duties because the law can generate associative obligations through its creation of a community of principle, then we will interpret law, if possible, in such a way that it does create a community of principle. I say more about Dworkin's theory of associative obligations in Chapter 7.

A weaker view is that law must be such as would justify its coercive enforcement, whether or not it provides subjects with genuine obligation. Thus in a recent article Philip Soper (2007) defends a moral filter view, according to which official directives that are so unjust that nothing could justify their coercive enforcement cannot count as law. This defense of "classical natural law" turns on the claim that law in its nature is not just that which the state presents as legitimate directives that can legitimately be enforced, but is that which can, in fact, be legitimately enforced. A state can justifiably enforce unjust law, but not grossly unjust directives. If the state does enforce grossly unjust directives, we are dealing with "acts of violence, rather than laws" – as Aquinas put it.

At the other end of the spectrum, it would be possible for a nonpositivist to believe, along with positivists, that the question of whether legal rights and duties are real moral rights and duties is always open – that the search for the content of law, though it is always informed by moral considerations, is not guided by the aim of finding real rights and duties.

Adjudication and Right Answers

As noted in Chapter 2, Dworkin's legal theory includes the further strong commitment that all normative considerations appropriately taken into account in adjudication are ipso facto among the grounds of law. This commitment is also not essential to nonpositivism as I have defined it. This is already plain from the discussion of the possible view that (only) formal rule-of-law values are among the grounds of law. On such a view, though moral considerations are always among the grounds of law, not all moral considerations appropriately taken into account in adjudication are within law's boundary. To take another example, suppose that the moral considerations always within the grounds of law relate only to matters of fundamental individual rights; considerations of social or economic justice, or of general welfare, by contrast, are excluded. Taking considerations of individual right into account in legal interpretation may still leave gaps, or indeterminacy in the law. A judge who resolves that indeterminacy by appeal to some theory of social justice or social welfare may be acting appropriately given her institutional role, on this possible view, but she would be in part making law, not just applying it.

It is tempting to connect the adjudicatory view with the "right answer thesis" – a yet further strong feature of Dworkin's theory. This is because it is natural to believe that there is always a right or best outcome to a legal dispute, even if we believe that the law itself is not sufficiently determinate to guarantee that. The adjudicatory view thus seems to go naturally together with the right answer thesis. But of course everything depends on the content of the theory of adjudication, on whether it has the resources to generate a unique best resolution to all disputes. Adjudication is plausibly thought always to yield a best answer if we assume that proper adjudication will help itself to unrestricted moral argument, even if that is not part of the determination of the content of law. For moral theory most obviously has the resources necessary to yield a single best result. That is not essential, however, since other theories of adjudication could also have adequate resources. If there were such a thing as "community morality," Cardozo's method of sociology would do the trick as well. As would some theory that holds, for example, that in cases of indeterminacy the defendant always wins. But the important point is that we should not assume that all theories of adjudication have the resources to guarantee a single best result.

The Moral Reading: Nonpositivist Puzzles

Dworkin's commitments to the right answer thesis, to the adjudicatory view of law, to the existence of a prima facie duty to obey the law, and to an unrestricted but appropriately structured (given those commitments) account of the moral considerations to be taken into account in legal interpretation – all these commitments hang together to form a coherent and well-motivated view. But it is important to emphasize that none of these commitments is essential to nonpositivism as I have defined it. In chapters that follow, I use "nonpositivism" in the minimal sense of a commitment to either the moral reading or the moral filter account of legal interpretation – and since it seems the better view, I will normally have in mind the moral reading.

Though it has roots in common-law legal reasoning (Perry 1987), the moral reading receives its best elaboration in Dworkin's discussion of legal interpretation in *Law's Empire*. We are to suppose a three-stage process. In the preinterpretive stage, we start with central cases, cases that everyone agrees are instances of valid law. This first stage involves no moral reasoning; preinterpretive law is a matter of brute fact. In the interpretive stage, moral considerations are brought to bear to find the general principles that best justify the past legal practice that produced those legal materials; legal rights and duties are those that flow from the best set of general principles that can be said to fit or explain past legal practice. In the postinterpretive stage, we may, on reflection, conclude that some of the legal materials identified in the preinterpretive stage are not legal materials at all; from the point of view of our interpretation, they are so far in tension with the best interpretation that they must be banished from law as mistakes. (Recall Blackstone: "For if it be found that the former decision is manifestly absurd or unjust, it is declared, not that such a sentence was *bad law*; but that it was *not law*; that is, that it is not the established custom of the realm, as has been erroneously determined.")

One important question is how far a good interpretation can go in declaring preinterpretive material to be mistakes. This is usually posed in terms of Dworkin's terminology of "fit" and "justification." The interpretive stage aims to justify past legal practice, but for it to do that, it must after all fit past legal practice; we would not be interpreting our law at all if we simply discarded all prior materials as mistaken. But how much fit is required? And to what extent can judgments of a required degree of fit be separated from the judgments of justification? These are important and fascinating questions, but a full discussion would take us too far afield here.[2] Let us simply assume that some plausible account of the twin tasks of fit and justification can be given that retains the dimension of fit as a genuinely independent criterion.

A somewhat different puzzle does need to be discussed here. It concerns the preinterpretive stage, the initial identification of legal materials that interpretation must (to some degree) fit. For this stage, the moral reading appears to require what we could call a provisional rule of recognition (Raz 1986). Provisional only because what is initially treated as a data point may of course later be expelled as a mistake. But the entire process depends on our ability to find considerable initial agreement about clear cases of valid law, which reveals at least some implicit convergence on criteria of validity. What's striking here is that

---

[2] See the extended debate between Dworkin (1985, 146–77; 1986, 65–8, 225–75) and Stanley Fish (1989, 87–119, 356–71).

nonpositivist legal interpretation takes as its object a matter of brute social fact; what we are interpreting is just what people agree, for whatever reason, is part of law. One way to criticize the view, understood in this way, would be to say that the moral reading takes legal materials that could have any content at all and pretties them up (Stavropoulos 2014 forthcoming). Why should we make the best of something that, so far as we know, initially has nothing going for it at all? The conviction that law is a location of value and a source of practical reasons seems to require more than that we make something morally indifferent look good. It would seem to require that we have some reason to think that there is value, or at least potential value, in the materials that interpretation must fit.

Now the situation is not as stark as this objection suggests. Procedurally valid statutory enactments are, in the moral reading, not *just* part of the brute facts to be fit; neither need the legal priority such sources have over judge-made law in common-law systems be treated as brute fact. For the practice of allowing representative institutions the final say over legal rights and duties (within limits) can itself be justified by democratic theory.

But suppose no such story were available. Suppose that legislation is made by lawmakers who inherit their roles; they have neither any claim to be representative of the people nor any special moral and political expertise. We may even suppose further that, substantively, the content of this legislation has systematically favored the interests of the hereditary ruling class. The idea that, when interpreting the law of this jurisdiction, interpreters should try to show it in its best light may seem entirely unmotivated. This relates to the problem of "evil law" for nonpositivists. If nothing good can be said about some legal tradition in the first place, the moral reading, the attempt to show that tradition in its best light, seems inappropriate. The natural response for the nonpositivist here is simply to embrace the conclusion that only certain bodies of preinterpretive legal material can generate legal rights and duties. Any collection of legal materials that lacks any seed of value, either in the manner of its making or its content, will simply be rejected as an appropriate site for legal interpretation. We could say that the moral reading must apply a moral filter to the preinterpretive legal materials, considered as a whole. I believe this is the most natural way to understand the moral reading (see Dworkin 1986, 101–13), and generally have this picture in mind in the chapters that follow.

In his latest writings, Dworkin (2006 34–5; 2011, 400–15) embraced quite a different approach.[3] Nicos Stavropoulos (2014 forthcoming) has introduced the terminology of "hybrid" and "nonhybrid" interpretivism that is helpful for making the contrast. The moral reading as I have so far laid it out corresponds to hybrid interpretivism. It treats legislative enactments or decisions of courts provisionally as sources of law just because everyone does (preinterpretive stage) – so long as they pass through the moral filter. At the interpretive and postinterpretive stages, such legal materials may be confirmed as part of the law, or not. On the reformulated view, it's a moral inquiry right from the start. The nonhybrid interpretivist approach treats legal materials as relevant to an investigation of what the law is *not* because everyone does, but because there is a good reason (if there is), grounded in political morality, to treat the past political decisions that produced those materials as sources of real rights and obligations. From this perspective, what we are looking for is not the content of some system of norms whose relation to morality is so far just that it has passed through a minimal moral filter; rather, when we look for the content of law, we are engaging in a moral inquiry at all times, seeking to determine what effect past political decisions of our political coercive order have on our moral rights and duties.

The first thing to notice about nonhybrid interpretivism is that it presupposes something that, as I have said, is not necessarily part of a nonpositivist view of the grounds of law, viz. that the outcomes of legal

---

[3] Stavropoulos (2014 forthcoming) and Greenberg 2011 hold that there has been no change; rather Dworkin has long been misunderstood. I disagree with that interpretation as, apparently, did Dworkin himself – see Dworkin 2011, 402.

interpretation are statements of real, moral, rights and duties and that this end point structures legal interpretation. Dworkin's reformulated view puts this position at the center of this theory of law. Legal interpretation just is a matter of figuring out what our moral rights and duties are, insofar as they flow from past political decisions.

So nonhybrid interpretivism is not a possible general account of the moral reading, since it depends on commitments that are not essential to the moral reading. But it is worth asking which view is preferable for those who accept that legal rights and duties are always real moral rights and duties. In one sense, nonhybrid interpretivism seems a clear improvement over Dworkin's original account of legal interpretation, since if we start with brute facts about what people think the law is, but insist that we end up with real rights and duties, it may seem obvious that the moral argument will always trump the brute facts. Though in the original account the dimension of fit is given moral significance through the value of integrity, or consistency in principle through time and across people, the morally salient kind of fit on that account is what has happened to people, rather than what people (even judges) have thought the law was (Dworkin 1986, 248, 284–5). This suggests that the reformulation was inevitable, as the original account left preinterpretive legal material with very little force in an interpretation driven by the final cause of determining real moral rights and duties.

On the other hand, if we drop any anchoring of the content of legal rights and duties in brute facts about people's views about the content of law, a new problem is immediately presented. Plausible moral arguments could be made that all kinds of past political (or social, for that matter) decisions and practices generate rights and obligations, but not all of them would ordinarily be identified as *legal*. Dworkin's solution to this problem is to say that legal rights and obligations are those that are appropriately adjudicated by courts (2011, 405–13). Given his commitment to the adjudicatory view of law, this is not a surprise, but it does come at enormous cost. Where actions of the executive or legislative branches of government are not appropriately reviewable by courts, they are by definition not subject to law, either domestic or international.[4] On the face of it, this seems an extremely high price to pay, for reasons I will go into in Chapter 7. It also seems to be a dogmatic and unmotivated piece of taxonomy, and for that reason inconsistent with Dworkin's idea (discussed in Chapter 6) that law is an interpretive concept.

More important, taxonomy is usually uninteresting, as Dworkin himself reminds us (2006, 4–5). Dworkin is not troubled by the fact that where some presidential decision is not properly reviewable by a court we must say that no legal obligations constrain the decision, since we can of course acknowledge the *political* obligations that apply (2011, 412–13). But if this is just a matter of labeling, the very natural next step is to say that it doesn't really matter which of the obligations people have in virtue of past political decisions get the label "legal" and which do not. In other words, I believe that this latest version of Dworkin's theory leads inevitably to the eliminativist position I discuss in Chapter 6. There isn't any such thing as law as a distinct normative system. There are just actions by various kinds of institutions that have moral consequences for the members of that political community.[5]

In any event, when referring to Dworkin's version of the moral reading in the remainder of this book, I have in mind his original account of legal interpretation from *Law's Empire* with all of its three stages.

Mistakes and Scorer's Discretion

Though there is of course much more that would need to be said to give a full account of the moral reading, I will end with just one further apparent puzzle. On the moral reading, judges can make legal mistakes by way

---

[4] Dworkin does not deny international law the status of law on account of the lack of international courts of general and compulsory jurisdiction. As he makes plain in (2013), his position is that legal rights and duties are those appropriately adjudicated by courts actual or hypothetical.

[5] These remarks apply equally to the positions laid out in Greenberg (2011) and Stavropoulos (2014 forthcoming).

of making moral mistakes. Thus if the death penalty really is, morally speaking, cruel, the moral reading requires us to conclude that the entire legal apparatus of the death penalty in the United States is based on a legal mistake; that it is, in fact, unlawful. This can seem to be an absurd result, as positivists sometimes insist it is (Marmor 2011, 91–2). But in fact the advantage of positivism over the moral reading in this connection is at best a matter of degree.

Any theory of law must account for the possibility of judicial error, and the possibility that judicial error may generate systematic application of that legal error by other judges and law enforcement officials. The alternative is a view of law according to which what the highest court says is law, is law. Hart criticized such a view by comparing it to a game of scorer's discretion – the rules of the game reduce to the decisions the scorer makes as there is no independent standard against which to criticize the decisions as mistaken (1994, 142–7).

A decision of the highest court is authoritative for the enforcement branches and lower courts until overruled or changed by statute. But though the application of the decision by other officials is in accordance with law, it may still have been a legal mistake. If what the highest court declares to be law is not only appropriately followed by lower courts and enforcement officials, but definitive of the content of the law, then there is no law, but simply a grant of absolute discretion to highest courts.

Both Hart and Dworkin recognize the importance of the possibility of legal mistakes in any account of law as a genuine normative system that effectively constrains legal decision makers (Dworkin 1978, 121; Hart 1994, 141–7). Both also, within the terms of their theories, can explain how what was once a mistake may become a source of law in the common law through the operation of the doctrine of precedent. This is familiar enough in the United States, where nominees for the Supreme Court frequently tell the Senate Judiciary Committee that though the decision in *Roe v. Wade* was a mistake, they would not overturn it given its entrenchment and consequent significant precedential weight. Hart (1994, 144) also notes the possibility that if we find ourselves concluding that most judicial decisions, most of the time, are mistaken, then the legal order – the complex set of rules that make up the content of the law in force on his account – would cease to be effective.

If there is to be a freestanding legal order that provides answers to legal questions, as opposed to an accepted practice of allowing judges to create legal rules without constraint, then any legal theory, positivist or nonpositivist, must accept into its account the legitimate enforcement of legally mistaken decisions. If there is an objection to nonpositivism here, it must be grounded on the assumption that if moral considerations are among the grounds of law, there is more scope for the institutionalization of judicial error than if they are not. But this assumption seems unwarranted, or at least in need of defense. The examples that make nonpositivism look silly – all those executions in Texas are contrary to law – naturally relate to legal issues with high moral stakes and prevailing moral disagreement. But there can be disagreement about the best way to understand a legal rule that does not turn on moral disagreement – as positivists in other contexts are eager to insist, in order to rebut the charge that on their view it must be true that everyone agrees what the content of the law is.

Thus take Lord Mansfield's argument, in a 1765 contract case, that

the ancient notion about the want of consideration was for the sake of evidence only: for when it is reduced into writing, as in covenants, specialities, bonds, etc., there was no objection to the want of consideration.[6]

This is an excellent argument against the idea that the doctrine of consideration called for a genuine quid pro quo. Sadly, Mansfield was reversed by the House of Lords in 1778,[7] and the requirement of an exchange remains part of the law in most of the common-law world.[8] The point here is that

---

[6] *Pillans and Rose v. Van Mierop & Hopkins* (1765) 3 Burr. 1663, 1670.

[7] *Rann v. Hughes* (1778) 4 Bro PC 27, 7 TR 350.

[8] Though outside the United States it has been largely undermined through judicial acceptance of the adequacy of a merely nominal exchange. *Chappell & Co Ltd v Nestle Co Ltd* [1960] AC 87.

this issue has enormous significance for legal practice; whether Mansfield and his brethren who joined him were right or wrong, lower courts were bound to follow his decision until overruled. Suppose he was mistaken about the proper understanding of the doctrine of consideration but he was not overruled. The common-law world would have rightly enforced a legal error – until the passage of time converted the error into good law, through the doctrine of precedent. Nothing in this example requires that Mansfield employed a moral reading of the existing legal materials. I venture that it is hard to determine in the abstract whether the moral reading is more or less likely to lead to the conclusion that "a great deal … of what people take to be the law … in a given legal system is legally mistaken" (Marmor 2011, 91–2) than a positivist approach to legal interpretation. A lot would depend on the content of the legal materials that are being read, and also the kinds of moral considerations that a particular nonpositivist view holds should be taken into account. I see no reason to find here a general objection to the moral reading.

Progress?

The disagreements between and among positivists and nonpositivists are stark. One main question in this book is whether there is any plausible way to resolve them. But it is important to start with a different question: Why have philosophers over the past two hundred years or so thought that this disagreement mattered? Why have they not been happy to allow what Aristotle appeared to take for granted, that there simply are different ways of referring to the category of law, and that this is a verbal dispute of only rhetorical significance?

Explaining why that is not so is our first main task. It will be useful to start by discussing what might be at stake in disagreements about the content of some other politically and morally important concepts.

5 Disagreement in Practical Philosophy

Throughout its history, up until the present, many have doubted that the dispute over what makes law is a substantive dispute. When Glanville Williams (1945, 146) said that this was "a verbal dispute, and nothing else," he was speaking for many others, before and since. My aim in this and the following chapter is to try to get some perspective on the distinctive kind of disagreement positivists and nonpositivists have, in order to see better both why they think it matters and what the prospects for progress might be.

One thing is clear – the disagreement is long-standing and convergence seems unlikely. But there are two cases to consider. Lack of convergence sometimes reflects a lack of genuine subject matter, or at least lack of important subject matter, and sometimes it does not. It is helpful to start by considering some apparently similar debates from moral and political philosophy (as does Dworkin 2006, 145–62).

Disambiguation

Persistent disagreement and misunderstanding about key normative ideas can be important in legal, moral, and political argument because of the ideological use to which conceptual entrepreneurship and the exploitation of unacknowledged assumptions can be put. Consider this discussion of liberty:

> A person does not exercise his liberties when he kills or enslaves another; he does not vindicate his property rights when he steals from

another. If he is restrained from these actions by another, he cannot claim a loss of liberty, but only the loss of an ability to act to which he was never entitled. Liberty is best understood as freedom from force or falsehood, not as a maximization of the things which are under one's disposition and control. (Epstein 1979, 489)

Three different notions of liberty are invoked here. There is the "rights definition" (Cohen 2011) of liberty as freedom to do what you like so long as you do not violate certain rights, the classical negative liberty of freedom from force, and a notion of positive liberty as maximization of things under one's control. What is important in this passage is the insinuation that the first two of these are equivalent, standing together against the rejected idea of positive liberty. Traditionally understood, negative liberty is interfered with by the enforcement of the rights and other legitimate claims people may have, and so it is unsuitable for libertarian slogans such as "liberty can be limited only for the sake of liberty." For that, the rights conception of liberty is more suitable. But "freedom from force and fraud" sounds more stirring as a rallying cry than "freedom from force except where force is necessary to enforce the legitimate claims of other people." So it is clear why a libertarian author might try to keep both of these ideas in the air at the same time, appealing to one or the other as the rhetorical demands of his argument require. And it is important for the critic to point out that different ideas or kinds of liberty are invoked, that the differences are important, and so on.

What doesn't seem important for arguments about libertarianism and for political philosophy generally is to settle what liberty, as opposed to some other possible political value, *really* is. Isaiah Berlin (1969, 121) was right to describe "liberty" as a "protean word." We can make sense of each of the three values, debate their relative significance and the connections between them. As a rhetorical matter, invocations of some of them may be more susceptible to demagogic abuse than others,[1] and the very fact that

---

[1] This seems to be the main concern Berlin (1969, ix) had about the concept of positive liberty.

there are these different but closely related (possible) values, all labeled "liberty," opens up the space for sleights of hand. So some may wish that a word of such historical significance were properly associated with but the one value. Certainly politicians and activists have reason to wish that in the public sphere it becomes associated exclusively with their own views.

It is also a substantive and worthwhile project to ask which notion of liberty people in a particular period of political history in a particular place have had in mind. Constant's 1816 essay comparing the liberty of the ancients and the liberty of the moderns is about something real and important, and discussions of this sort are entirely familiar in the history of philosophy.

But what doesn't seem plausible is to insist that there is but the one liberty and that there is an important philosophical disagreement about just what the contours of that value are. All the important philosophical and normative issues remain if we always specify more precisely which value – liberty as lack of interference, liberty as autonomy or self-actualization, liberty as respect for and enforcement of some list of rights, liberty as freedom from domination, and so on – we mean to discuss.[2] Even if all accounts of liberty are connected at a deep level – they are, perhaps, different views about the most important ways a society can promote or hinder human agency[3] – it is nonetheless clear to everyone that there is a range of fairly well-understood potential values here; argument over which one really deserves the splendid label "liberty" seems inevitably just strategic, aimed at rhetorical advantage. It is hard to see a substantive dispute here.

Persistent Superficial Disagreement: Democracy, Justice, and the Rule of Law

The case of democracy seems different. Arguments about what democracy really is do not seem so obviously empty. This is because there isn't

---

[2] Chalmers (2011, 532) calls this the "subscript gambit" – we have liberty$_1$, liberty$_2$, liberty$_3$, and so on.

[3] I am grateful here to a suggestion made by Alan Ritter.

a well-recognized range of fairly clear accounts of different ideals for
governance that we imagine people might have in mind when they talk
about what is democratic, and what is not. Debates about what democracy really is seem, on the face of it, to be substantive debates about the
content of the same ideal, not just strategic arguments to claim a politically powerful word for their own cause.

There's a good amount of agreement about what democracy is. A
democracy is a system of governance where the people rule, in some sense.
The people rule, rather than, say, a monarch, or an oligarchy, or a political
party. Though some insist that there is no democracy without substantive
equality, pretty much all agree that rule by philosopher kings who aim
at securing equality is not democratic. Nor was the German Democratic
Republic democratic, despite the fact that the use of the label in 1949 to
claim the antifascist tradition in German history was understandable, as
a political gambit. So there is some level of agreement about the features
all democracies share. Beyond that, there is disagreement, and some of it
seems intractable. Is any derogation from majority rule a derogation of
democracy? Is judicial review of legislation democratic? Is democracy
possible in a society of gross social and economic inequality?

These intractable disagreements strike me as superficial, in that pursuing them doesn't matter terribly much to the main projects of political philosophy.[4] Of course, disagreement about democracy can provide
a space for instrumental argument similar to that we observed for the
case of liberty. Everyone wants their preferred ideal of governance to
be thought of as democratic, and it is important to be aware that disagreement about the main features of democracies may open up space
for rhetorical maneuvering.[5] So it is important that we are aware of this
disagreement; and there's a practical reason why it would be better if we
didn't disagree.

---

[4] Scanlon (1998, 371–3) makes a similar point about disputes about what it means to
   have a (practical) reason.
[5] Dunn (2006, 15) asks: "Why should it be this word that has won the verbal competition
   for ultimate political commendation across the globe?"

But our interest in knowing the nature of democracy is, I believe, purely theoretical in the sense that it isn't necessary for us to have a view about this before offering a theory of legitimate or just government. It is the possible contribution of democracy to legitimacy that gives debates over what democracy is their main importance. Debates over judicial review are best understood as debates about whether constitutional arrangements that include this feature are more or less legitimate, or otherwise choice worthy, than arrangements that lack it. This is the important question of political philosophy that "democratic theory" can contribute to, and we don't need to think about the nature of democracy in order to make progress with it. We can continue our discussion by talking about the values of self-governance, political voice and political liberty, the epistemic or instrumental value of majority voting, noting also the possibility that none of these things will secure equality or the protection of minority and other rights, and so on. Since those are the important questions, and we don't need to have a view about the nature of democracy to address them, it is natural to think that the latter debate is trivial, even purely verbal.[6]

On the other hand, it could be said, the fact that there are these underlying important issues connected with debate about the nature of democracy proves the exact opposite – that the debate is substantive and important (Dworkin 2006, 145–62; Gallie 1955). There is a generally promising strategy to be found here: in the face of apparent stalemate about the right account of some X the two sides might be brought back to the table when they reach agreement that whatever else X is, it has such and such features, or is connected with some other ideal. They can then perhaps find that there is agreement about the features, or the other ideal, that in turn has implications for the nature of X.[7]

---

[6] This proposal for "democracy" is an application of what Chalmers (2011, 526) calls "the method of elimination."

[7] As we will see in the next chapter, both Dworkin and Raz employ this strategy in their arguments about the nature of law.

So for the case of democracy, we might think that we can move forward by agreeing that whatever else it is, democracy is the best or most legitimate or otherwise choice-worthy system of government. Kelsen (2000, 104–9) noted that much early twentieth-century theorizing about democracy implicitly took this form. However, he believed that this was an objectionable strategy; he thought it clear that it was not of the essence of democracy that it was the best system of government. The history of philosophical discussion of democracy, mostly critical until the seventeenth century at least, certainly shows that Kelsen's belief has been widely shared (Dunn 2006). The important point here is just this: of course, if it is taken for granted that an argument about the nature of democracy just is an argument about the best system of government, it is easy to see that it is an important and substantive question what democracy is; but that just makes clear that it is the question of what the best form of government is that matters – and not whether that will always count as a democracy.

We seem to be in a very similar situation with respect to justice. In the opening pages of *A Theory of Justice*, Rawls writes:

> The concept of justice I take to be defined, then, by the role of its principles in assigning rights and duties and in defining the appropriate division of social advantages. A conception of justice is an interpretation of this role. (1999, 9)

This is Rawls's version of Hart's (1994, 159–60) idea that all accounts of justice tell us to treat like cases alike, while different accounts of justice vary in their criteria for likeness. Rawls and Hart held that so much is fixed by the very concept of justice. Neither took the claim to be controversial or requiring any kind of argument in its defense. What they were doing, in effect, was setting the parameters within which they believed all substantive argument about what justice requires would take place.

Of course, it is possible to disagree with Hart and Rawls about those parameters, or to offer more restrictive ones. Take the issue of whether it is unjust that most residents of the countries of the global North enjoy high levels of welfare while many residents of the global South live in desperate poverty. Some believe that this is a grave injustice while others argue that, though the world's rich have humanitarian obligations to the world's poor, the situation can not accurately be described as unjust. One form of the argument goes like this. Justice is concerned with the importance of equality – of relative and not just absolute levels of well-being. But the moral significance of relative levels of well-being emerges only within a single political society, so it follows that there is no global injustice.[8]

Once again, it is clear that what matters here is the right account of our obligations, individual, collective, and political, for the absolute and relative welfare of others, domestically and globally. In my view, we should not get hung up on what justice requires, as that might just mask the fact that we already agree on the important issues.

But the same strategy tried out for democracy is possible here as well. It might be said that whatever else justice is, it specifies a set of moral demands on governments that have a higher priority than other demands. There is an important distinction, in other words, between mere obligation, the right thing to do, and obligations of justice. If all sides accept this, then argument over justice will just be argument over the content of the weightiest demands political morality applies to government. That's an important debate. But once again, not everyone will agree that this is just the same question as what justice is. And others, such as utilitarians, will deny that there is any such moral hierarchy. What all sides accept is that we need to discuss what the obligations of individuals, collectives, and governments are, domestic and international; argument about where justice fits into all that again just seems to get in the way.

Take next the ideal of the rule of law. On most people's understanding, the rule of law is a political ideal that stands opposed to arbitrary and

---

[8] Nagel (2005, 119) writes: "Humanitarian duties hold in virtue of the absolute rather than the relative level of need of the people we are in a position to help. Justice, by contrast, is concerned with the relations between the conditions of different classes of people, and the causes of inequality between them."

personal rule. As Waldron (2002, 157) well puts it, the general aspiration is that of "law being in charge," and a debate is then to be had about how that might be possible and what the best form of government through law might be. Many of us think of the rule of law as an ideal that can be satisfied even though the content of the law is grievously unjust or otherwise bad, and also that satisfaction of the ideal does not guarantee legitimacy. For us, that's the whole point of this ideal; it sets out the conditions under which a system of governance by law can achieve a distinctive good – distinct from justice and legitimacy – just in virtue of being that kind of system of governance (see Raz 1979 for the classic statement of this position). But others, especially in recent years, associate the ideal with a particular substantive content to law – for example, robust private property rights, or that which will in fact justify the use of force in the law's name.[9]

Figuring out what the rule of law is might seem to matter an enormous amount. Not just legal theorists and political philosophers but also politicians and development economists tell us that we should promote the rule of law (Davis 2004; Waldron 2007). But there are, as we've seen, two ways this kind of dispute can matter. It is obviously essential in the case of the rule of law to be aware of the different implications attached to this ideal by different people. Here the risk of ideological sleights of hand is even more evident than in the case of discussions of liberty and democracy. Some claims about free markets and the rule of law should obviously be ignored because they are avowedly made in bad faith.[10] But it is a fairly well-established minority view that the entire discourse of the

---

[9] For critical discussion of the former, see Waldron 2007; the latter view is exemplified in Dworkin's work over many years.

[10] Here is the World Bank in its report on "Rule of Law as a Goal of Development Policy": "The main advantage of the substantive version of the rule of law is the explicit equation of the rule of law with something normatively good and desirable. The rule of law is good in this case because it is defined as such. This is appealing, first because the subjective judgment is made explicit rather than hidden in formal criteria, and, second, because the phrase 'rule of law' has acquired such a strong positive connotation." Quoted in Waldron (2007, 118).

rule of law is hopelessly ideological, and so the only sensible thing to do is stop talking about it altogether (Shklar 1998, 21).

The second way the disagreement can matter is that it would be good to make progress with it, because it relates to an important question, something we'd like to know the answer to. But, as with democracy and justice, I believe that what makes the issue of the rule of law important in this second sense can be fully accounted for by shifting our debate to other issues. We should discuss the values of procedural fairness, effective enforcement, the separations of powers, the constraints a mode of governance must satisfy if it is to respect subjects' agency, and so on. And if we did that while leaving the rule of law to one side, we would liberate ourselves from the tiresome need always to check just what particular set of values an economist, politician, or political theorist is hoping to slip by us by using a label we all associate with only good things.

Persistent Substantive Disagreement: Wrongness

I have been arguing that much of the persistent disagreement about democracy, justice, and the rule of law can be seen as superficial because all sides can agree to a reframing of their debate in more fundamental terms, where there is every possibility of agreement being reached. Of course, there is also every possibility that persistent disagreement will continue. The progress we will have made, however, is that all sides will agree that it is those more fundamental debates that really matter and we will have avoided the confusions and opportunities for manipulation that disagreements at the superficial level introduce. It is tempting to say that we have revealed any remaining disagreement about justice, democracy, and the rule of law to be purely verbal, or disputes of meaning. But that is to take a stand in a wider debate about what distinction can be drawn between questions of fact and questions of meaning that would not be necessary for my purposes.

To complete the picture, consider someone who believes that the only consideration that is relevant to determining right and wrong conduct is the impact on aggregate welfare. Starting from this statement, there should be a lot to say by way of continuing the argument. The nonutilitarian points out that on the utilitarian view, it's hard to see why it would not be morally all right to kill one person to distribute his organs and save five lives. If the utilitarian responds by saying that this is, in fact, all right because it would maximize welfare, the debate could still continue because the opponent would continue to produce reasons that count against the view that welfare is all that matters morally. Human rights, for example, are not easily explained in welfarist terms. And what about the fact that it seems almost absurd to say that we are all morally required to continue trying to benefit others, whomever and wherever, up to the point where the cost to us would equal the benefit to the others? This substantive argument could go on forever.

Disputes about right and wrong obviously matter. And unlike the cases of democracy, justice, and the rule of law, there are no other debates in the neighborhood we can turn to without substantive loss. There is no case for saying that the kind of dispute set out in the previous paragraph is superficial, or purely verbal. So here we appear to have reached bedrock; our vocabulary is exhausted (Chalmers 2011, 543). The disagreement is persistent, and it matters in the second, substantive way – we would hope to make progress with this disagreement, hope to be able to get the matter right.

Legal Texts

Persistent disagreement about democracy, justice, and the rule of law can be seen as superficial since we can continue the argument by discussing other, closely related values. If we are not doing political theory but instead interpreting legal texts, our constraints are different. Article 7 of the Canadian *Charter of Rights and Freedoms* provides that

> Everyone has the right to life, liberty and security of the person and the right not to be deprived thereof except in accordance with the principles of fundamental justice.

An interpreter of this text will have to make judgments about what liberty and justice are for the purposes of Canadian law. Neither requesting clarification about which value "liberty" is meant to pick out, nor sidestepping an investigation of what justice is, are options. But while the constraints are different when justice and the rest are invoked in legal texts, the resources are richer as well. If the interpreter is a judge, and the legal system follows a principle of stare decisis, either explicitly or implicitly, past decisions will narrow the scope for disagreement considerably. And if it is a case of first impression, or the clause in question is not apt for adjudication by a court, other resources can be found in the best theory of interpretation for that legal system. Legislative history, for example, or its equivalent in the constitutional context, might appropriately be consulted to narrow the range of plausible options. It is a consequence of these differences that justice or liberty in the legal context may turn out to be rather different ideals than they are outside that context. This is not news, of course – we need think only of the ideals of due process and equal protection in the context of U.S. constitutional law.

Law

When philosophers debate the grounds of law, they are not interpreting any particular legal text. As the Lawyer said to the Philosopher in Hobbes's *Dialogue*, there is no definition of law in any statute. So we have to confront the question of whether the dispute about the grounds of law is like that about the nature of democracy, justice, and the rule of law or instead like that about wrongness.

In the next chapter, I'll take very seriously the eliminativist position that law is just like democracy, justice, and the rule of law. We don't need to argue about what law is or what makes it, on this view, since we don't need to know the content of the law in force. We can get along perfectly well by talking instead about how judges should decide cases, how governments should act, and what the state is likely to do to us if we act in various ways.

But I will defend the view that law is instead like wrongness. Law is a bedrock item in our social lives. Something is lost if we try to substitute for disagreements about the content of law related but different disagreements about what judges should do, and so on. The dispute about the grounds of law matters, and it matters substantively. This makes it worthwhile trying to figure out how we might make some progress with it.

6 Law

The Instrumental Approach

We noted in the previous chapter that political theorists and politicians prefer to have accounts of liberty, democracy, justice, and the rule of law that help persuade others to their overall point of view (Gallie 1955). The same is true for law.

The range of politically significant issues tied up with the question of what can and what cannot be counted as a ground of law is great (for further discussion, see Murphy [2001a, 2005]). Depending on whether we embrace positivism or nonpositivism, it could be argued that we the public will be more or less likely to believe that there is a prima facie duty to obey the state's commands or believe that its rule is legitimate; will have greater or lesser respect for the state; or will be more or less concerned about the legitimacy of judges' appealing to moral considerations in the course of making decisions. There is also a range of possible effects on legal officials of various kinds. Perhaps we get better outcomes from conscientious judges if they are not positivists (Dyzenhaus 2010); or perhaps it is the other way around.

If we are convinced that general convergence on a positivist or nonpositivist account of the grounds of law will produce one or more of these effects, and if we already have views about the desirability of these effects, that will give us a reason to wish for that convergence, and reason to urge others to reform their understanding of what law is. At least until

1961, when *The Concept of Law* was published, Hart was clearly thinking along these lines:

> If we are to make a reasoned choice between these concepts, it must be because one is superior to the other in the way in which it will assist our theoretical inquiries, or advance and clarify our moral deliberations, or both. (Hart 1994, 209)

So Hart was prepared to defend a positivist account of law on essentially instrumental grounds.

It is common to reject this approach by saying that it confuses what is with what we would like to be (Dickson 2001, 84–93; Raz 1980, 215–16; Waluchow 1994, 86–98). But the instrumentalist can cheerfully claim, as Frederick Schauer (2005) does, that even if there were convergence on a univocal concept of law, it could still be appropriate to argue that we would be better off embracing a different one. Hart and Schauer are not confused: the instrumental argument is not about what the content of the concept of law really is, but rather about what it would be best for it to be. In Carnap's (1947, 7–8) terms, they offer an explicative definition of "law" – one that preserves much of the meaning the word has in ordinary use, but extends or refines it for the sake of certain ends.

I prefer to characterize this approach as urging us to redirect our attention from the law, that thing we have been disagreeing about, to something else. For Hart and Schauer, the thing we should be thinking about is what we might call positivistic law.[1] The idea seems to be this. Consider all the contexts in which it has been thought important to know what the law is. In all those contexts, it would be much better if we all agreed that what mattered was positivistic law, not some other thing, such as, in particular, nonpositivistic law.

There is, I believe, a plausible nonspeculative case to be made that exclusive positivism tends to promote a healthy critical attitude to the

---

[1] In effect, they employ Chalmers's subscript gambit (see chap. 5, n. 2).

state (Murphy 2001a, 2005).[2] The basic thought here is well expressed by Kelsen (1973, 92), who writes that nonpositivism "tends towards an uncritical legitimisation of the political coercive order ... for it is presupposed as self-evident that one's own political coercive order is an order of law." But the argument that positivism or nonpositivism will lead to better judicial decisions needs to consider a wide variety of possible situations, turning on the many possible permutations of the variables of the goodness or badness of existing law and of each branch of government. And there are the other possible effects to consider. Even if there were agreement on the appropriate ends for the instrumental argument, it would pretty clearly not be possible to establish the descriptive part of the argument – that either positivistic or nonpositivistic law will do better, all things considered.

Furthermore, the right aims themselves seem to depend on circumstances. A critical attitude to the state seems obviously desirable in stable and more or less homogenous polities such as Norway for the past hundred years, but it is hard to deny that in particular times and places, a quietist attitude to the state may be for the best. One option is, of course, to accept that the instrumental argument for the best substitute for law is inevitably parochial. I have heard it suggested that justice was well served in the civil rights era in the United States by a quietist attitude to the (national) state. Should we have different recommendations for, say, Canada and the United States, saying that Canadian judges applying Article 7 of the *Charter* must always in part make positivistic law while American judges applying the equal protection clause never make nonpositivistic law? Whatever may be the importance of either a quietist or a critical attitude in any given circumstance, this seems like a bad result.

Suppose, against all hope, that the instrumental argument worked on its own terms: one or another substitute for law would do best, all things considered, in all circumstances. The most fundamental problem

---

[2] For a fuller account of why the instrumental approach no longer seems viable to me, see Murphy (2008), on which my discussion here draws.

remains. The instrumental argument is that convergence on the preferred new object of inquiry and concern would have good effects; if there is no convergence, we don't get the good effects. The fundamental problem with the instrumental argument is that there would never be convergence because we don't all agree about the ends we should be aiming at. It makes no difference that there may be a correct answer to the question of which are the most important political ends; being correct doesn't mean that others will agree with you. And if we don't all agree to start talking about positivistic (or nonpositivistic) law rather than law, nothing is gained.

Why the Grounds of Law Matter

Though the instrumental approach to the dispute over the grounds of law has no promise, both its initial appeal and its failure highlight the importance of the perceived political implications of different ways of understanding the relation between law and morality to any explanation of why this has seemed worth fighting over. For my own case, certainly, distrust of what can seem overly romantic views about law explains my instinctive attraction to positivism (Murphy 2001a). Even those who have insisted all along that there is no sense in looking for a stipulated substitute for law can agree that one reason this particular philosophical project is engaging is that its conclusions may have politically significant consequences.[3]

But without more, the political stakes of the debate over the grounds of law show only that the debate matters in the first, negative way identified in the previous chapter. Different accounts of democracy, justice, the rule of law, and the grounds of law all have political implications. All of these debates matter in the sense that we need to know that there are these different accounts abroad, with importantly different political implications, and so we need to be on the look out for ideological fudging.

---

[3] The best example of what I have in mind is Raz (1994, 194, 221).

If I am right, however, only the debate about the grounds of law also matters in the second, substantive sense.

As we have seen in Chapter 2, we need a view about the grounds of law if we are to be able to figure out the content of the law in force. Though positivists and nonpositivists share a lot of beliefs about law, it is equally clear that these different views about the relation between law and morality will lead to variations in judgments of legal validity. This is not a variation we can simply shrug off. We are happy to say that on some views about what democracy is, judicial review makes a constitutional regime less democratic while on other views it does not. But we are not happy saying that on one understanding of what law is, same-sex couples have the legal right to marry while on another they do not. The problem is not with the idea that some legal questions have no determinate answers; incomplete or vague sources make this a commonplace, at least from the positivist point of view. The problem lies with the idea that there are simply different fundamental pictures of what law is and that these different pictures will yield different answers to particular questions about the content of law. At least initially, the natural thought is that one of these views about the very foundations of law must be right.

Of course, a theory of the grounds of law only matters if it matters whether we can find out the content of the law in force. But on the face of it, it seems obvious that it does. Law matters not just for the evaluation of the state but also for the day-to-day operations of its main institutions and for people's understanding of their day-to-day interactions with it. Whatever else it does, law governs the categorization of rules and standards into those that are presented by the state to its subjects as legitimate demands and those that are not. Many people also accept the law as reason giving. Law, it seems, has great everyday importance for all of us.

Which makes it all the more disheartening that the prospects for progress with the dispute over the grounds of law are poor. Those dim prospects will justify a second look (later in this chapter) at the possibility that we don't need to know what the law is. In the meantime, I will try to explain why the disagreement between positivists and nonpositivists seems so intractable.

Analysis of the Concept of Law

The traditional view has been that we approach the problem of the grounds of law by providing an account of the content of the concept of law. This has remained the prevailing view over the past half century, despite the controversial status of conceptual analysis within philosophy during much of that period. In the previous chapter, I argued that disagreement about the nature of democracy, justice, and the rule of law was in the end unimportant because we can discuss all the important issues associated with those values without discussing the values themselves. Chalmers (2011) is inclined to conclude from this kind of result that the original debates were *verbal* – simply disputes about meaning or the content of concepts, and for that reason of no philosophical interest. I have not taken a stand on whether my conclusion that such disagreements are unimportant supports the conclusion that they are merely disputes about meaning. I will also not take a stand on whether the dispute about the nature of law is best understood as a dispute about the content of a concept as opposed to a dispute about the most fundamental facts about law. What I do believe is that all the arguments philosophers have made about how we should figure out the content of the concept of law can be rephrased as arguments about what the most fundamental facts about law are.

There are several familiar methods for pursuing the analysis of concepts, each of them importantly different from the others. They all nonetheless share a central feature: at the foundations, they depend on intuitions about the proper application of the concept in particular cases. These intuitions about correct usage can equally well be interpreted as judgments about what these ideals require or how to resolve uncertainty about that. As a result, the distinction between factual and conceptual disputes, or the philosophical issue of whether there is one, can be left to one side as we investigate the dispute between positivists and nonpositivists.

The traditional way of analyzing concepts used answers to well-posed questions as the data from which to build a list of necessary and sufficient conditions for correct application of the concept. Is this legless thing that carries people up mountains a chair? Is a speed limit the kind of thing that could be just or unjust? Is a country where less than half of the population votes in national elections a democracy? Can I be free if I have nothing to eat? Is this striped, vicious marsupial a tiger? In recognition of the difficulty of finding a list of necessary and sufficient conditions, there is the alternative of seeking a "cluster" of defeasible descriptions (of whatever the concept is a concept of), explicit or implicit knowledge of which would suffice for mastery of the concept. Legal philosophers have tended to follow Nicos Stavropoulos (1996, 2) in referring to such an approach as "criterialism."

The main rival approach that legal philosophers have been attracted to is the "causal-historical" approach that ties the reference of a term to the nature of the thing in the world that was first given that label. This view is supported by thought experiments such as Putnam's (1975, 215) question about whether a substance on "Twin Earth" that satisfied all the descriptions we on earth commonly associate with water, but which had a chemical structure other than H_2O, would be successfully referred to in the utterance of "water" by an earthling. The correct intuitive response is supposed to be no, and this is the basis of the idea that the extension of the concept of water is fixed by the nature of the thing (as discovered by science) called water by the first user of the term and those who followed him, not by any cluster of beliefs ordinary people have about water. Most philosophers seem to share Putnam's intuitions here whenever the concept concerns a "natural kind." But not all do, and nonphilosophers are apparently divided on the matter.[4]

---

[4] For discussion of divergent intuitions about this kind of thing, see Weinberg, Nichols, and Stich (2001); Segal (2004). I myself have no confident intuition one way or the other about this case. Kripke's (1980) examples concerning biological kinds are more

It seems that the causal-historical approach to the concepts I have been discussing, including law, doesn't get off the ground. This approach requires for its support intuitions about cases just as much as the criterialist approach (Fodor 2004; Jackson 1998, 31–42; Mackie 1974). But it is hard to think of the right kind of example, since there is not, for the case of democracy and the rest, the same plausibility to the distinction between underlying structure or essence and superficial description that the examples concerning natural kinds turn on. We don't have even a tentative account of the essence of democracy that is sufficiently distinct from a folk description to serve the purpose that molecular structure does for the water example. But suppose it were plausible to believe that descriptive political theory, "at the end of inquiry," would produce an account of the essential nature of different systems of government. Suppose, in other words, that the problem here is just the poor state of contemporary political theory. Then support for the causal-historical theory could come from a more abstract or theoretical kind of intuition – an intuition that the extension of the concept of democracy is to be found by uncovering the nature of those systems of government to which the

approachable; for example, we are invited to agree with him that a reptile that looks just like a tiger is not in fact a tiger and wasn't one even before we had developed our modern biological taxonomy. I find Kripke's invitation resistible, at least when I think about real cases rather than hypothetical ones. The thylacine, now extinct, was first called a Tasmanian tiger because of her stripes. Later it was considered more correct to call her a Tasmanian wolf, because she did, in fact, look and act a lot like a wolf. Biologically speaking, the thylacine was no more a wolf than a tiger; she was a marsupial. But then there is, it seems to me, a broad sense of "wolf" where it is perfectly reasonable to distinguish between placental and marsupial wolves. My intuition here is that the broad sense of "wolf" was always there – it did not get coined for the first time when someone first saw wolf-like marsupials; but I'm sure many disagree with that. So even for terms referring to things that might be thought to have a scientific "essence," the intuitions supporting the causal-historical account of reference are, I think, unstable and therefore cannot be the basis of a refutation of a criterialist approach for such concepts. It is therefore perplexing that some philosophers appear to believe that intuitions about natural kind concepts support the rejection of a criterialist approach to any concept, and so too to such politically significant concepts as that of the cruel and unusual (Brink 1988) and law (Coleman and Simchen 2003).

term "democracy" has been applied in a causal chain since the initial baptism – where that nature may have nothing to do with the kinds of beliefs that guide people in their day-to-day use of the term. The trouble is that this is an intuition that very many of us, both philosophers and ordinary folk, do not have. This is hardly surprising, when we consider just how far our ideas about the system of government "democracy" picks out differ from those of the ancient Greeks (Dunn 2006).

Stavropoulos (1996) applies a version of the causal-historical approach to the case of law – the reference of "law" is fixed by what legal experts tell us about the nature of paradigm cases of law. He offers a sophisticated and detailed argument against objections to extending the causal-historical model to legal concepts, but his view in the end must still be grounded in intuitive reactions to cases. Once more, it is hard to see that this grounding will be forthcoming. Supposing that the relevant experts are lawyers and legal theorists, we know that, unlike the chemists who tell us about the nature of gold, they don't all agree about the nature of law.[5] But suppose that the experts did agree; the main point is that there are clear limits to the deference ordinary folk are willing to extend. Suppose that the experts all agree that law is in its nature a rational normative order and that allowing civilians to possess military assault weapons is irrational, and therefore such possession is contrary to law everywhere. It is possible that some residents of the United States would react to this news by revising their beliefs about the content of the law in force; most would not.

---

[5] A point Coleman and Simchen (2003, 22–7) make against this view. But the view they favor is no more plausible. They put forward a version of the causal-historical approach according to which the reference of "law" is not determined by what the experts tell us about the nature of the paradigm cases. Rather, "to fall under the extension of 'law' is to bear the appropriate similarity relation to paradigmatic instances. But the determination that something or other bears this similarity relation to a paradigmatic instance of law is a task that the average speaker can be expected to be able to carry out" (27–8). But insofar as there is supposed to be a determinate extension for "law," there needs to be just the one similarity relation. Just as the experts disagree about the nature of law, we ordinary folk disagree about what the relevant similarity relation is.

By contrast, the criterialist approach does get off the ground, since reflection on our concepts will yield *some* criteria we share, at least of a negative kind – an absolute monarchy is not a democracy, for example (see Raz 2001, 2005). But when it comes to the questions that really matter, such as whether derogation of majority rule is, to that extent, a derogation of democracy (a question that might be approached by asking people whether a system of parliamentary sovereignty is more democratic than one with judicial review), we will get no agreement.

Applying the criterialist approach to the concept of law, the hope would be to come up with a list of (perhaps defeasible) criteria for its correct application generally accepted in the relevant population. Of course, the idea is not that such criteria are already consciously embraced in the population, but that general acceptance would emerge from imaginative philosophical argument. But it seems certain that, for our question of whether the content of the law can be determined in part by moral considerations, there will be no convergence at the level of criteria, because there will be no convergence at the level of example. Could there be a valid law of racial slavery in the United States? No, say some. Yes, say others.

Robert Alexy (2002, 35–9) in effect invokes the criterialist approach with his idea that legal statements include a "claim to correctness." He gives the example of a constitution that announces in its preamble that it establishes a sovereign, federal, and unjust republic. Such a text would be making a "performative contradiction," as the "claim to correctness – in this case as, above all, a claim to justice – is necessarily attached to the act of framing a constitution" (37). He notes that "X is a just state" is also conceptually odd, if found in a constitution, as it seems redundant. But it is just as plausible to conclude that all this is conceptually fine; after all, the positivist may say, there are unjust constitutional orders and everyone knows that. The example is just politically odd: since states present their law as legitimate demands on the subjects, why would the founding documents tend to undermine that posture? It is akin to a university having as its slogan, "X – A second-rate university."

As I have emphasized, the disagreement between our two camps seems both deep and primitive, and so it is not surprising that it shows up at the level of particular cases.

It is precisely to this situation of persistent surface-level disagreement that both Dworkin and Raz respond by offering methods of conceptual inquiry that mix the descriptive and the normative.

Raz's (1988) "normative-explanatory" account of the concept of authority is normative in the sense that it takes a stand on substantive issues that have been contested politically and philosophically. Raz therefore does not claim that anyone who has mastered the concept of authority implicitly believes his theory of authority. But the account is also meant to be explanatory in that it is "an attempt to make explicit elements of our common traditions" that singles out "important features of people's conception of authority" (65). For Raz, the normative and explanatory aspects of his theory together amount to "a discussion of a concept which is deeply embedded in the philosophical and political traditions of our culture" (63). The idea here is that brute disagreement about usage is not the end of the matter – substantive argument can continue in the form of moral argument about what legitimate authority would look like. And yet we remain engaged in the project of understanding the concept we all share, in order better to understand ourselves. As Raz (1994, 221) puts it: "It is a major task of legal theory to advance our understanding of society by helping us to understand how people understand themselves" (for discussion, see Bix 2005; Murphy 2007).

Dworkin (2006, 2011) insists that "conceptual analysis that does not involve normative judgment, assumptions, or reasoning" (2006, 146) is not part of constructive political philosophy. The main concepts of political theory, such as those we have been discussing, and including the concept of law, should be seen, in his view, as "interpretive concepts": concepts whose deep structure can be revealed only by a constructive interpretation of the practice in which the concept finds a place. Such an interpretation aims to find a point to the practice, and to characterize the value picked out by the concept in its best light. In effect, we settle disagreements about what democracy really is by arguing about what it is about democracies that is worth having. Since this process is normative – it is, in fact, doing political philosophy – we can expect to come up with a correct or best account.

The problem with these mixed methods is that, like every other method of conceptual analysis, they are hostage to convergence in intuitions about particular cases – here we need intuitions that can support the generalization that the proper application of these concepts emerges from a political theory about the values they pick out. Dworkin believes that we have such convergence: we share a practice of arguing about what (say) democracy is that shows a shared implicit commitment that "what a democracy is depends on which political theory provides the best justification of paradigms of the concept" (2011, 163). My response to this is hardly deep – it's simply that I think that there is no implicit agreement derivable from the way we debate particular cases that the right way to figure out the content of the concepts of democracy or authority or law is to engage in substantive political argument. I for one would never have been in the least bit tempted to defend a view about what democracy *is* by arguing that my account offers the best justification of some paradigm case.

Consider, as an example, Dworkin's (1996, 1–38; 2011, 379–99) discussion of democracy. According to Dworkin, most people mistakenly associate the concept of democracy with majoritarian institutions. He makes the powerful point that if we do that because we believe that what is central to democracy is self-governance, we need to recognize that there are substantive preconditions of equality that would have to be met before a society could rightly be said to be governing itself through majoritarian institutions. But even supposing that I am convinced by this argument that majoritarian institutions are not in themselves valuable, this does not in the least shake my sense that the concept of democracy is centrally tied up with the existence of such institutions. In other words, this argument doesn't change my understanding of democracy as a *category* at all, even though it may alter my thoughts about its value.

The point to emphasize from this discussion is that all accounts of the content of particular concepts will in the end need to be grounded in intuitions about proper usage. If we cast our discussion as one about the facts – the nature rather than the concepts of democracy, and so on – what I have been calling intuitions about usage are just considered judgments about the nature of democracy, law, and so on. As my own preference is to understand the dispute about the grounds of law as a clash of foundational beliefs about the nature of law, I continue the discussion in those terms.

Arguments for and against Positivism

As I noted in the previous chapter, when we seem to be at loggerheads in discussion about what X is, it seems a generally promising strategy to argue as follows. We seek agreement that whatever else X is, it has such and such a feature; we then give a plausible account of that feature that we can also agree on; last, we point out that this has implications for the nature of X. This is in essence the approach both Raz and Dworkin take to the debate about law, though they couch it, as I have said, in terms of conceptual analysis.

Raz's (1994, 194–221) celebrated argument connects law with authority. The initial premise is that law claims authority. Simply stated like this, without any further specification of what authority is, this seems like a very plausible claim. There may be quibbles about what it is for something like law to make a claim, but I think the idea is nonetheless rather clear and compelling (for helpful discussion, see Gardner 2012). I wrote earlier that it matters what the law is because the law, whatever else we can say about it, is presented by the state as a legitimate demand. Modifying this to accommodate law beyond the state, we move somewhat closer to Raz's formulation: the law presents itself as a set of legitimate demands. Whether what law demands of us is something we ought to do, in any sense, may remain an open question, but all sides to the debate about the nature of law should be able to agree to this claim about how law presents itself, or is presented by the political coercive order through its officials. What we are looking for is a way to get beyond a degenerate "Yes it is/No it isn't" kind of argument, a space in which new substantive considerations can be presented; this thought about law and legitimate demands or directives promises to do just that.

So Raz's argument starts with a question: "Do you agree that law claims authority?" "Yes," we are all supposed to answer. "But then you see," the argument goes on, "that that means that it would be very odd to think that moral considerations in part determine the content of law, since if we have to figure out the moral issues on our own, the law couldn't serve as an authority, since an authority is precisely someone or something that can figure out what you ought to do on your behalf, and do a better job." We see now that it turns out to matter very much that I have agreed that law claims *authority*, in the precise sense of being able to tell me what my obligations are, and not just that it is a source of legitimate demands. That leaves me starting to feel unsure about the argument's first step. And I'm even less sure once I realize that I am supposed to think that what law claims is authority understood in light of Raz's theory about when authority would be legitimate – when it can do a better job figuring out my reasons for action than I can myself (see also Murphy 2007). I don't think that the law claims any such thing, and I can't actually imagine ever coming around to the view that it does.

It seems even less likely that anyone drawn to a nonpositivist view about law would come around. Raz's account of authority, which may or may not be the best political theory of what would have to be the case for a person or institution or state actually to have legitimate authority, will evidently be very unappealing as an account of the (potential) normativity of law to anyone initially attracted to nonpositivist views. If you see the content of law as in part a moral question, this account of what law does if it can tell us what our obligations are is obviously incompatible with your picture of law. Of course, that's why the argument would, if successful, establish positivism. But working through the example of Raz's argument suggests the possibility that no theoretical argument about features associated with law will ever carry as much conviction as do the basic positivist or nonpositivist pictures for those in their grip.

Dworkin's argument for his nonpositivist account of law also approaches the nature of law by reflecting on the nature of a value it is said to be associated with. Whereas Raz holds that law claims authority, Dworkin holds that where there is law, there the value of the rule of law, or legality, is satisfied:

> Claims of law are claims about which standards of the right sort have in fact been established in the right way. A conception of legality is therefore a general account of how to decide which particular claims of law are true. (2006, 170)

This claim seems to me implausible on its face. Many theorists (such as Raz [1979, 210–28]) have explicitly claimed that the rule of law and law are not coextensive, and that seems intuitively right, to me at least.

But perhaps the connection between law and the rule of law is inessential for Dworkin's argument.[6] His fundamental idea (rephrased to remove the conceptual framing) is that to figure out the nature of justice, democracy, law, and so on, we have to figure out what is good about those values. We get democracy right by figuring out what would make democracy most valuable. We offer an interpretation of the value and the practice that appeals to it that presents the value in its best light. Similarly, though law isn't just a value, for Dworkin it evidently has value, and so for law we must offer an interpretation that presents what we take to be good about law in the most compelling way: we present the value associated with law as the best or most choice-worthy value it could be, while still being the value associated with law. Again, we could object that, for some people, there is no value associated with law as such. Certainly this is the way Hart thought about it (1994, 249). But even leaving that aside, the invitation to figure out the nature of law by thinking about what

---

[6] When a version of the claim is made in Dworkin (1986, 91), he adds that his argument does not depend on it.

would make law seem best is fairly obviously deeply unappealing to any-one who has any kind of attraction to the positivist picture. The positivist is likely to say that trying to make law look good is precisely what she is against; in fact, it is the importance of a cool, detached, stance toward law that motivates her positivism in the first place.

So we don't seem to have progressed very far from our accounts in previous chapters of positivism and nonpositivism as two different fun-damental understandings of the kind of thing law is. It's not that the two camps each think that the other side is missing something. Each side thinks that the other is fundamentally and hopelessly mistaken about what law is. For the reasons given, I am skeptical about the availability of substantive argument that might have the power to move either side closer to the other. All the arguments I have seen inevitably include some premise or methodological commitment that is sure to seem less compel-ling to one of the sides than their initial fundamental convictions about the kind of things law is.

I am not arguing that there is no truth of the matter about the nature of law. What I believe is that the disagreement in this case is stark and fundamental, and does not seem to connect sufficiently to other matters we care about, or at least not in the right way, to make substantive argu-ment possible.

Eliminativism

The standoff is hardly surprising for those who all along have thought that our dispute was purely verbal, that the two sides are merely using the term "law" in different ways and that's all there is to it. What has made this conclusion seem implausible is the simple thought that the dispute about the nature of law must be important because it is impor-tant to know the content of the law in force. Unlike the case of democ-racy, it hasn't seemed that we do just as well talking about adjacent issues and leaving the content of law aside. But perhaps we should now reconsider.

The proposal that we should simply stop talking about the content of law is more radical, though more plausible, than the proposal that we should replace talk about law with talk about, say, positivistic law. The suggestion is that, in place of inquiry into the content of the law in force, we need nothing at all.[7]

Of course, there is no chance that people will stop talking about what the law is, so the proposal really amounts to the claim that this talk plays no important role in legal practice and social life generally – it is a wheel spinning on its own. We can get on perfectly well by discussing a range of other questions. Within legal practice, judges and other legal officials need a theory of legal decision making, which is a political theory setting out what textual materials and other considerations it is appropriate to take into account and in what way. As we saw in Chapter 2, such an account can be expressed without reference to the content of the law in force prior to the decision; it is entirely possible for positivists and nonpositivists to agree about the best theory of adjudication. Legal practice also requires a theory of legal counsel, of how lawyers should advise clients. This is where Holmes's (1897) "bad man" theory of law can seem plausible: Lawyers should advise clients on the assumption that all they care about is how the legal system will affect their interests and so offer predictions about what it is most likely to do to them if they make certain choices. Whether or not the "bad man" description is necessary, the idea that lawyers do and should advise clients based on predictions about what will happen, as opposed to considered judgments about the content of current law, is not novel. Finally, considering legal practice in the broadest political sense, we need a theory of what legal systems should strive for if they aspire to realize good governance. In addition to legitimacy and justice, there are the distinctly legal issues associated with the ideal of the rule of law, such as the separation of powers, procedural fairness and respect for the agency of subjects, along with questions of legal

---

[7] My account of eliminativism emerged out of many conversations over nearly two decades with Lewis Kornhauser. See Kornhauser (2004) for his own framework.

design such as whether it is better for legislatures and judges to produce texts and pronouncements made up so far as possible of formally realizable rules.[8]

We can say and do a lot with these accounts of legal decision making, legal counsel, and good governance. What we cannot do is discuss what the law now is: any such question must be paraphrased into a moral question about what a person ought to do or a descriptive question about the state's likely responses to people's decisions.

We need not try our hand at eliminativist rephrasings of familiar discourse about law. For even if coherent paraphrases were available for every familiar kind of claim about the law, it would not be plausible to think that nothing important had been lost in the translation.

As I have said, law governs the categorization of rules and standards into those that are presented by the state to its subjects as legitimate demands and those that are not. For the criminal law, in particular, it seems ridiculous to propose that, properly understood, there are no crimes, just good or bad decisions in criminal cases and better and worse predictions about our interactions with the criminal justice system. There is, at the very least, an expressive significance to the criminal law that this redescription cannot capture. Consider the situation in Singapore with respect to Section 377A of the *Penal Code*, which criminalizes sex between consenting adult males. In a 2007 speech to Parliament opposing repeal of this section, the prime minister of Singapore announced that the government would not "proactively enforce" it.[9] Does that mean that gay men in Singapore have nothing to complain about until

---

[8] The issue of design is the one that "normative positivists" are most centrally concerned with. See Campbell 1996, 2004, 2005; Waldron, 2001, 2009a. Methodologically, Campbell embraces the instrumentalist approach: we should stipulate the concept of law that, among other good effects, fits best with the model of law as a set of formally realizable rules (2005, 27). One possible interpretation of Waldron's "normative positivist" articles has him embracing a version of Dworkin's interpretive method. This method is explicitly embraced in Waldron 2008, 47 n. 143).

[9] Lee Hsien Loong speech's to Parliament http://www.yawningbread.org/apdx_2007/imp-360.htm.

the government changes its mind and starts prosecuting gay men for having sex?

But more important than law's expressive function is the role of law in people's practical lives. Consider first the legal subjects that are the typical focus of legal philosophy – individuals in more or less well-functioning states. Many people "accept" the law in Hart's sense: for some reason or other, they treat valid law as giving them reasons for action. The point Hart wanted to make with his notions of acceptance and the internal point of view was that for many or most people, legal norms do not simply set prices on possible actions, where the price varies from context to context. We do not typically deliberate about the costs and benefits of following the law "for this case only," but adopt a standing policy about the reason-giving force of law in general. This standing policy might, but need not, be based on a sense of moral obligation. We might, for example, accept legal norms out of a sense of self-interest or a mere preference to conform with the conduct of others.

Suppose that I accept legal norms out of a belief that, in general, my life goes better if I comply. If all I am worried about is the effect of my compliance on my own welfare, it might seem that I would do better with a Holmesian theory of legal counsel than a theory of law. What I need to know is how my welfare will be affected if I do certain things, and since legal norms are not magically enforced, that might suggest that I need a predictive theory about the behavior of judges and the executors of law. So if concern with my self-interest leads me to accept the law, the eliminativist may claim that I am making a mistake, that the rational thing to do is regard legal rules as setting prices for particular decisions.

This is not, however, an obviously compelling claim, since it may well be that I generally do better simply following the law as I understand it rather than deliberating about the effects of compliance in each particular case. This seems particularly evident when we take into account reputational factors, the good that comes my way, as I might plausibly believe, from being generally regarded as a law-abiding character. I cannot reliably predict or control these effects, nor the success of efforts to conceal noncompliance. So a sensible course would be to adopt a deliberative "rule of thumb" according to which I will follow the law unless some special reason presents itself to me that might justify my taking the time to think about whether I would in fact do better not complying in a particular case. Now of course whether all this makes sense will depend on the circumstances. If I am very badly off without a career to protect, the Holmesian approach may well be appropriate, since relatively speaking I have more to gain from certain forms of noncompliance and reputational effects are less important to my welfare. But if my circumstances are fortunate, the gains from noncompliance in particular cases will not, relatively speaking, be so important. If I can assume that other people, officials and ordinary legal subjects alike, have mostly the same views about the content of law as I do (or will form after I consult a lawyer), it cannot be asserted a priori that it is irrational to accept the law for self-interested reasons.

Suppose now that I accept legal norms because I believe that they are morally binding. Here too it could be claimed that I am confused. Isn't what I should be concerned about rather the judicial decision that authoritatively declares my legal duties and rights? So wouldn't I actually get closer to my goal of performing my legal obligations if I accepted instead the outputs of good adjudication, actual or hypothetical?[10]

We consider the strength of the moral reasons there in fact are for accepting the law in the next chapter. But supposing for now that there are moral reasons to accept the law, the question is whether anything would be lost if people instead treated as reason-giving good legal decisions, what those with authority to resolve disputes ought to decide. For those who accept the adjudicatory view of law that would in any case be equivalent to treating the law as reason giving, since on that view the law just is what a judge, acting in her professional capacity, ought to base

---

[10] I am grateful here to Lawrence Sager.

her decision on.[11] But for positivists and for nonpositivists who reject the adjudicatory view, the proposal would obscure something of importance: the ability to be able to say, for example, that while I accept the law as it is, I believe that the courts ought to overrule the relevant precedent or invalidate what has until now been valid legislation. It is an important aim of positivists to bring to the surface (what they regard as) the fact that judges have the authority to change the law. It is not as if is this idea were exactly revolutionary, at least in the common-law world. Sometimes even judges announce that they and the litigants before them are bound to one set of norms (current law) though the case for the highest court to reach a different decision (and thus change the law) is strong. The adjudicatory view implies that the norms we do or should accept are those that would properly be announced by a highest court even in cases where we have little reason to expect that a highest court will address the issue and every reason to expect that lower courts will, in conscientiously carrying out their professional roles, recognize different norms (see Waluchow 1994, 31–79 for relevant discussion).

This brings out that the very issue of the grounds of law, as opposed to the theory of adjudication, has clear significance for those who reject the adjudicatory view of law, but unclear significance for those who accept it. Another way to bring this out, in terms of Dworkin's theory, is as follows. For Dworkin, when an individual is trying to determine the law for his own case, his process of deliberation should be exactly the same as a judge's. Each of us has the responsibility to interpret the legal materials to show them in their best light. We do not defer to authority on the content of law – thus the characterization of the theory as "protestant" (1986, 190). What this means, again, is that what individuals need to know is precisely what judges need to know if they are conscientiously to discharge their obligations when resolving disputes. It is therefore not surprising that Dworkin's (2011, 404–5) latest view identifies the legal with

---

[11] We can leave aside cases where the law is so bad that the judge has moral reason to abandon her professional obligation to reach a decision in accordance with law.

the justiciable, holding that legal rights and obligations just are political rights and obligations that "are enforceable on demand in an adjudicative political institution such as a court."

But all that is impossible to accept if there can be a difference between good interpretation of the law and good adjudication, since if that is so judges must be recognized as having law-making power that individuals of course do not have. An individual must figure out what the law is, not pretend he is a judge. In many cases, for those who reject the adjudicatory view, a conscientious individual and a conscientious judge can and should reach different conclusions.

The upshot, as with just about every other issue that connects to that of the grounds of law, is that the question of eliminativism looks different depending on what theory of law we are inclined to accept. Perhaps the adjudicatory view of law is correct, in which case we could greet the eliminativist proposal with shrug. But for those who reject that view, the eliminativist invitation to replace acceptance of law with acceptance of the outputs of good adjudication must be rejected too.

Let us turn next to the kind of legal subject much less often discussed by legal philosophers – states.[12] As I argue in the next chapter, states or governments are the morally most important subjects of law, in the sense that the normative significance of law is clearest for them. For now, however, the issue is how the eliminativist challenge looks when applied to the case of states as legal subjects.

Law that applies to states rather than individuals includes international law, constitutional law, and ordinary domestic law such as legislation that applies to the executive branch of government. As Chapter 8 is devoted to the additional issues raised by international law, I restrict myself here to domestic law.

A government may ignore the law, and (we hope) concern itself with good governance alone. But a government, or its officials, may also accept

---

[12] See Goldsmith and Levinson (2009) for closely related discussion. I am grateful to David Golove in this and the next few paragraphs.

the law. Would they do as well accepting the outputs of ideal adjudication? In some cases, with the details depending on the legal system in question, the situation of a branch of government subject to law is similar to the situation of individuals subject to law. Courts or other adjudicatory bodies may be available to review, to a greater or lesser extent, executive and legislative interpretation of applicable law. However, in all legal systems there will be limits to the justiciability of legal questions that relate to government action. Even in a legal system with liberal rules of standing and a willingness by courts to consider "political questions," institutional factors – such as the ability to collect the relevant information – inevitably limit the kinds of legal issues that courts can competently address. And even apart from legal doctrine that limits courts' adjudicatory role, there is the simple fact that a legal issue may not end up in court, for all kinds of extralegal pragmatic reasons. So the question arises of how nonjudicial branches of government should approach the matter of determining the content of the law that applies to them. The implication of the eliminativist suggestion to drop law and make do with a theory of adjudication is that the legislative and executive branches should deliberate about their legal own situation as if they were adjudicating disputes.

Once again, if we accept the adjudicatory view of law, the question will not arise. There is only one interpretive task to be found, and that is the same whether the interpreter is making a decision about the law for someone else's case or for her own case; and if making a decision for her own case, it makes no difference whether the subject of law is a private individual or an official of the state acting in a professional capacity.

By contrast, if we reject the adjudicatory view of law, a number of interesting political questions must be confronted. Should the legislature, when attempting to confine its law-making activity to the constraints of a constitution, reason about what is and is not permitted in exactly the same way as a court charged with constitutional review of legislation? There is a current discussion in the United States about extrajudicial constitutional interpretation. One issue is whether judicial interpretation, where present, should govern (Alexander and Schauer 1997; Whittington 2009).

Along the way, several questions arise about the differences between the two kinds of interpretation such as whether legislatures need give no weight to their own precedent – prior legislative interpretations of the constitution.

Similar questions arise for the executive branch deciding whether the Constitution allows, for example, a certain military action. Suppose that this is not considered a justiciable issue and that a plain reading of the constitutional and legislative materials leaves the question unsettled within a certain range, in the manner of a Kelsenian frame (1967, 350–1). Should past constitutional understanding by officials of the executive branch carry weight? Must the government attempt to settle the issue by carrying forward the principles that it can uncover in the Constitution and relevant legislation (as interpreted by courts?), or should it treat the Kelsenian frame that the texts provide as a space for entirely free choice so far as the Constitution is concerned?

And if the courts give deference to statutory interpretation by an administrative agency, should the agency see its interpretive task as the same that a court would have if it were not deferring?

In every one of these three cases, it is just as implausible to suggest that the legal interpreter has the authority to change the law as it is for the case of the individual subject. This is because of the obvious difference between determining the law of one's own situation and resolving a legal dispute between third parties.

Another important general point is that whether or not there is a doctrine of stare decisis, courts are thought to declare the law at least for the particular case. This is a precondition of taking precedent seriously. It also supports the thought that indeterminacy left by a plain reading of the legal materials should be resolved by courts in a way that is true to discernible underlying principles – in the manner of Dworkin's theory of interpretation – rather than by way of legally unconstrained choice. It is obvious that the conclusions of private individuals about their own legal situation should not be treated as declarations of what the law is that has weight for others. For the case of governmental legal subjects this is not obvious. It is an open normative question whether the conclusions of the executive and/or the legislature about the law that applies to them should be treated as authoritative declarations about the content of law as applied to the particular case, or instead as good faith attempts by these branches to comply with the law as they see it.

In a recent study of the role of precedent in the executive branch in the United States, Trevor Morrison concludes that the Justice Department's Office of Legal Counsel does to a large extent follow its own precedent. More important for current purposes, however, is his normative analysis. Morrison argues that precedent should have weight for the executive branch, but a different weight than it should have for courts. On the one hand, decisions concerning executive power should have greater precedential weight, especially when in line with past executive practice; on the other hand, the views of the Office of the President about the content of current law should have special precedent-trumping weight. "The argument here rests on the President's democratic accountability and his ultimate responsibility for the actions of the Executive Branch" (2010, 1511).

But perhaps the most telling difference between judicial and executive legal interpretation in Morrison's analysis is his understanding of the president's responsibility in the face of a controversial legal issue.

> Although his oath of office obliges him to uphold the Constitution, it is not obvious he would violate that oath by pursuing policies that he thinks are plausibly constitutional even if he has not concluded they fit his best view of the law. It is not clear, in other words, that the President's oath commits him to seeking and adhering to a single best view of the law, as opposed to any reasonable or plausible view held in good faith. (2010, 1466)

This does amount to the view that the executive can choose within a Kelsenian frame, so long as the borders of that frame are set by plausible interpretation of the content of current law.

The issues raised here are obviously very complex, and their detail depends on the content of constitutional law and institutional arrangements in a particular jurisdiction. My point is the very general one that eliminativism would make it impossible to discuss what appear at first glance to be significant political/legal questions. The fact that they make no sense on the adjudicatory view of law would seem to impugn that view rather than the questions.

As a final point, it should be noted that my discussion thus far of "theories of adjudication" has been too simple. As Lewis Kornhauser (unpublished manuscript) convincingly argues, we tend to think about adjudication on the model of an appellate judge sitting alone, whereas in fact what we need are theories of adjudication appropriate for trial judges sitting alone, on the one hand, and appellate judges sitting on collegial courts, on the other. Moreover, different actual collegial courts have different practices for announcing decisions – thus English collegial courts issue opinions of individual judges seriatim, while U.S. collegial courts offer a majority opinion, together with possible concurrences and dissents. Which kind of collegial court a judge sits on will affect what will need to be taken into account in reaching a decision. If differently positioned judges need different theories of adjudication, the eliminativist suggestion is underspecified: Which kind of judge are we all supposed to be imitating when we try to figure out the content of the law?

In light of all these points, an eliminativist could concede that we need more than a single theory of adjudication, a theory of legal counsel, and a theory of good governance. We will need multiple theories of adjudication for different kinds of courts. We may also need a variety of theories of proper legal interpretation; these theories will set out how different kinds of legal subjects (private individual, legislator, executive official, and so on) should figure out what rights and obligations they have in virtue of extant legal materials. Conceding all that is consistent with the position that no one needs to know what the law is. Just as judges don't need a theory of the law to resolve disputes, but rather a theory of factors to take into account when discharging their obligation to resolve disputes, other legal subjects need only an account of how legal materials that apply to them affect their moral rights and duties. If each of us is equipped with an account of the moral significance (for someone in our position) of statutes, constitutions, and so on, there is simply no need to answer the further question of what the law is.

But by now the whole thing is starting to seem implausibly artificial. The natural thing to say about the range of nonadjudicatory contexts I have discussed is that different legal subjects may stand in different relationships to the law that is in force, both in terms of the normative implications of the law for them, and in terms of the effects of their decisions about how to behave on the further development of the law. For judges too, the most natural way to express the various theories of adjudication that the variously positioned judges will need will be in terms of their different relationships to the law that is in force.

Perhaps the most compelling way to bring this out is to consider the position of lawmakers, legislators and judges alike.[13] If no one ever needs to reason from beliefs about the content of the law in force, lawmakers should no longer think that what they are creating are legal directives or facilitating legal rules. Rather, the materials lawmakers create are the grounds of moral arguments for individuals and officeholders about their rights and duties as partially determined by legal materials, where, moreover, those arguments take a different form in each case – individual, executive official, adjudicator, legislator. It's not clear exactly what the lawmaker should have in mind when thinking about how to improve the legal materials.

To put the eliminativist proposal in perspective, it may be helpful to compare the case of law to something else that philosophers have generally thought plays an essential role in moral argument – the idea of a person's overall welfare (or well-being). Utilitarianism holds that we ought always act so as to promote overall welfare. And any plausible moral theory will tell us that we are sometimes required to make people's lives go better (some people's lives, to some extent, and so on). It would seem, then, that any plausible moral theory requires a freestanding

---

[13] These thoughts were prompted by Smith 2011.

theory of welfare. There is a considerable literature addressing the question of what the best theory of welfare is. The familiar options include experiential, desire, and substantive good theories (Parfit 1984, 493–502; Scanlon 1998, 113–26). Experiential theories tie welfare to having subjective experiences we prefer (pleasure and freedom from pain), desire theories to the satisfaction of actual desires, and substantive good theories to the achievement of certain goods that would include pleasure and the absence of pain but also such things as close relationships, success in our rational aims, appreciation of art and nature, intellectual development, and so on – where some of these things may be taken to be good for us whether or not we desire them. It would seem that figuring out the right account of welfare is essential if we want to know how to live well, either morally or prudentially.

However, Scanlon (1998, 108–43) has raised a kind of eliminativist argument about welfare. Just as our eliminativist argument about law argues that we don't need a freestanding theory of the content of law to figure out the obligations that are in part determined by legal materials, Scanlon argues that we don't need a freestanding theory of welfare to figure out our moral responsibility to promote the interests of others or to figure out how to act in ways that are good for ourselves. The argument is complex, but the gist of it is that while we can invoke a notion of welfare in our practical reasoning, it is typically neither necessary nor the most direct way to proceed. When it comes to our own case, we do just as well, or better – since the contours of welfare are not clear – reasoning directly about the various factors that constitute welfare; we don't pursue our rational aims, for example, because they contribute to our welfare, though they perhaps do that. Similarly, from the third-person perspective, if we have reason, moral or not, to be concerned with the welfare of others, it is plausible that not all aspects of what makes a person's life go better according to the best theory of welfare are our responsibility. In either case, it seems that a theory of welfare need not play any role in our reasoning.

I believe that Scanlon approaches the issue in exactly the right way. The issue is whether there is a significant practical role for the theory of welfare. If there is not, there may be such a thing as a person's welfare, but we need not trouble ourselves trying to get it right. As it happens, I think that Scanlon underestimates the practical role of judgments of welfare in a number of ways. To give just one example, it seems that though parents should be concerned with the aims and aspirations of their children even beyond any contribution to their welfare, parents ought nonetheless to think that their primary responsibility is to do what they can to promote all aspects of their children's welfare. Figuring that out requires thinking about what really does make a person's life go better overall. This applies at the political level as well. A department of child welfare is aptly named. And when a family court judge decides a custody dispute according to the welfare or best interests of the child, she does need a notion of what exactly that amounts to. So though not all third-personal responsibility for the interests of others encompasses the whole of the welfare of others, some instances of that responsibility do.

I might be wrong about whether practical deliberation would be impoverished without the idea of welfare; Scanlon may be right that it would not be. I mention welfare as a comparison case because it does help bring into focus what is at stake in the issue of whether we need a theory of law in our practical deliberations, or whether, by contrast, law is an abstraction that we can bypass by going directly to the moral significance for people in particular positions of certain political facts, such as that a legislature has passed a certain directive.

As I have said, there seem to be two main reasons why we continue to need a theory of law. First, debates about how different legal subjects – individuals, legislators, executive officials, (differently positioned) judges – should respond to legal materials are most naturally understood as debates about how people in these positions may stand in different relationships to the law that is in force, both in terms of the normative implications of the law for them, and in terms of the effects of their decisions about how to behave on the further development of the law. Second, and perhaps more important, is the fact that lawmakers cannot plausibly be thinking that what they create are political facts that have a variety of implications for a variety of different kinds of legal subjects. For there to be any coherent and manageable structure to the thoughts of those who create law, they must be thinking that they are creating directives to be presented to all relevant subjects as legitimate demands on their conduct.

A Problem?

So we seem to face a problem. We cannot give up on the idea that it matters what the law is, but disagreement about the grounds of law runs so deep and is so tenacious that we frequently have no option but to say that on one not unreasonable understanding of the nature of law, the content of law is such and such, but that on another, it is something else. Though this situation may not be terribly troubling in other areas of inquiry, where we might just cheerfully accept that there is much disagreement abroad, the role of law in social life makes it troubling for this case in particular. It is especially troubling that the persistent disagreement does not come from case-by-case differences in judgments about how to apply various generally accepted criteria to particular cases, but rather from disagreement about what those criteria are. Disagreement about the very grounds of law, stemming from profoundly different views about the kind of thing law is, seems incompatible with the role of law in structuring the relationship of subjects to the state and through it, to each other.

Of course, I haven't proved that this standoff is permanent; there's no claim that greater convergence is impossible. The most promising general strategy would be to continue to search for agreement about the relation between law and something else where reflection of the nature of that something else might provide reason to embrace either positivism or nonpositivism about law. Though I have said that the versions of this approach offered by Raz (law and authority) and Dworkin (law and legality) are unsuccessful, I certainly haven't shown that no version of this approach will succeed. Nonetheless, I am in the end inclined to think that our two camps are unlikely ever to be moved by argument – no other considerations are going to strike them as more compelling than their initial pictures of the nature of law. It's a bit like the standoff between a profoundly committed utilitarian and his non-welfarist opponent. Whether persistent lack of convergence in ethical beliefs should be a cause of philosophical concern is disputed. Some say this casts doubt on moral realism, others deny this. But in the case of law, the problem is not (just) that lack of convergence may raise doubts about there being a truth of the matter to the content of law. Lack of convergence in beliefs about the very foundations of the content of law matters in a more pragmatic way in that it seems inconsistent with the role most of us assign to the law in our deliberative and social lives.

Agreement about How to Figure Out Law's Content Despite Disagreement about the Grounds of Law

The different role assigned to moral considerations in our two accounts of the grounds of law means that sometimes productive argument between the two sides about a legal proposition will not be possible. In Chapter 2, I gave the example of same-sex marriage in New York.

Might the two views about morality and the grounds of law always result in disagreement about the content of law, at least in the United States and other countries where individual rights are constitutionally enshrined?[14] Some people believe that the equal protection clause of the Fourteenth Amendment to the U.S. Constitution enacts, as part of U.S. law, a moral principle of equal treatment: "government must treat everyone as of equal status and with equal concern" (Dworkin 1996, 10). Others believe that the equal protection clause authorizes the Supreme Court to decide, outside the boundary of law, whether legislation or common-law doctrine violates its view of what morality requires in the domain of equal protection. As decisions are made, and to the extent that the principle of stare decisis is taken seriously, a body of equal protection law builds up.

---

[14] The next several paragraphs are closely based on Murphy 2005.

But certainly, the positivist will say that right after Reconstruction there was very little in the way of a law of equal protection.[15]

As there is no agreement on the right way to understand the equal protection clause, and as all law must satisfy that clause, do we not face the result that all legal argument will run into this foundational disagreement? Take a piece of legislation that is not unconstitutional on a nonmoral reading of the Constitution and Supreme Court precedent. Assume also that on the best moral reading of equal protection, the legislation violates this right. A positivist holds the legislation valid, a nonpositivist holds it invalid. And there is no evident argument available that might resolve the disagreement because it depends not on competing interpretations of the legal materials, but on different views about whether moral considerations are among the grounds of law.

But still – equal protection clause or no equal protection clause – it is not the case that disagreement about the grounds of law always leads to different conclusions about the content of the law. No one thinks that ten years imprisonment for murder is unconstitutional in the United States, or that the law against murder violates the law of equal protection, or that only marriage between persons of the same sex is permissible under New York law. Though some insist that these conclusions depend in part on moral reasoning and others deny it, agreement on the truth of these propositions doesn't depend on agreement about why they are true. And of course there is in any case partial agreement about why they are true. Positivists and nonpositivists agree a great deal about the grounds of law. It is not just that they may end up with the same conclusions about

[15] The exclusive positivist position is succinctly brought out in this passage of Raz (1994, 217): "If the argument here advanced is sound, it follows that the function of courts to apply and enforce the law coexists with others. One is authoritatively to settle disputes, whether or not their solution is determined by law. Another additional function the courts have is to supervise the working of the law and revise it interstitially when the need arises. In some legal systems they are assigned additional roles which may be of great importance. For example, the courts may be made custodians of freedom of expression, a supervisory body in charge both of laying down standards for the protection of free expression and adjudicating disputes arising out of their application."

particular legal issues. They agree also about a good many of the factors that are relevant to reaching such conclusions. All sides agree that legal sources such as validly enacted statutes, judicial decisions, and constitutional provisions are among the sources of law.

Of course there are disagreements about how to interpret such legal sources and what weight to give them. But again, in a significant range of cases, those favoring moral readings of sources, and a moralized approach to the doctrine of stare decisis, can end up in the same place as positivists who offer a straightforward nonmoral interpretation. Nonpositivists agree that legislation imposing a sentence of ten years for murder is constitutional because there is no plausible moral case that this amounts to cruel and unusual punishment; and the criminalization of murder does not violate the equal protection clause because there is no plausible moral case that it fails "to treat everyone as of equal status and with equal concern." Sometimes the moral factors that nonpositivist accounts of law locate within the boundary of law are inert, even if they are always in principle playing a role.

Suppose that a plaintiff in a contract case argues that his letter containing an offer of a world cruise for $15,000, "deemed accepted if we don't hear from you within 10 days," created a binding contract once the ten days had expired, though the offeree had done and said and intended nothing. The rule that there is no contract in a case like this is well established in unambiguous common-law precedent, and the moral case in favor of the plaintiff's point of view is extremely weak. If we follow Dworkin and try to interpret contract law as a whole to show it in its morally best light, there is simply no case for concluding that the offeree is legally bound.

Now it is in general true that the less determinate the legal materials and the less agreement there is on issues of interpretation and the weight of precedent, the more the moral factors recognized by nonpositivist accounts of law will have a role to play. Since indeterminacy in the sources and standards for interpretation and the weight of precedent makes for less law on the positivist view, it is tempting to think that disagreement about the grounds of law is relevant if and only if we venture into the territory where the positivist believes that there is no determinate answer to the question of what the law is. If so, that would seem to be some kind of vindication of the positivist approach. Sadly, it's not so. In this example from contract law determinacy in the legal materials coincided with low moral stakes. But that is not always the case.

Take the issue of damages for breach of a contract for which there is bargained-for consideration. Here the rule that expectation damages is the default remedy is as well established in clear precedent as anything in the common law. But from the moral point of view, there is actually a lot to think about. Contract theorists argue endlessly about whether the default remedy should instead be reliance damages, specific performance, or something else. If we take a moral reading of contract law as a whole, it could be plausible to conclude that contract law (already) provides for, say, the more general availability of the remedy of specific performance, despite the fact that this would force us to conclude that many prior conclusions by judges about contract law were mistaken.

Still, it is true that on any plausible nonpositivist view determinate guidance from extant legal sources considerably constrains the inquiry into what the law is; so even when the moral issue is a live one, determinacy in the source law will affect the degree to which disagreement about the grounds of law is engaged.

It is important that what I am saying does not collapse into the view that the law is what everyone agrees is the law.[16] There can be considerable disagreement about the content of the law even when everyone agrees about all the relevant factors to take into account. Was Judge Easterbrook right to say that § 2–207 of the Uniform Commercial Code did not apply to a case where there was only one contractual form?[17] There's a substantive debate to be had, since, in the context of this statute, we all agree that the ordinary meaning of the statutory text, read as

---

[16] I thank Shelly Kagan for pressing me on this.
[17] *ProCD* v. *Zeidenberg* 86 F.3d 1447 (1996).

a whole and along with interpretive precedent, provides the answer to this question. Much of the common law of contract is technical in this sense too. Does the law of a particular state accept the view of §87(1)(a) of the Restatement (Second) of Contracts that: "An offer is binding as an option contract if it ... is in writing and signed by the offeror, [and] recites a purported consideration for the making of the offer"? Either the law includes this formal device or it does not. Even if it would be good to have it, morally speaking, that can't mean that it is already there if there is no trace of it in prior case law. But whether the prior case law contains enough of a trace of it to conclude that it is a legally effective way of making offers irrevocable can be a matter for substantive debate.

One More Time: Does Disagreement about the Grounds of Law Matter?

We can continue to engage in productive argument about law even though there is widespread disagreement about whether moral considerations are among the grounds of law. But there are a number of legal questions where different views about the grounds of law will lead to different conclusions about what the law in force is – in some places, such as the United States, there are a large number of such questions, and many of these are very important questions. Does this matter? Lawyers can still give predictive advice and judges can use their theory of legal decision making without worrying about whether, in doing so, they are applying or making law. And for citizens too, the realization that in *some* cases the best we will be able to say is that on one understanding of the kind of thing law is what happened was contrary to law, but on another understanding it was not, may not matter very much so long as this kind of stark standoff about how to figure the content of law is not the typical case. It is one thing to say that, for some subset of legal propositions, profound disagreement about the very kind of thing law is leads to different answers to the question of legal content; quite another to say that this is the case for all or most legal propositions.

We do need to know what makes law because we need to know what the law is. As it happens, however, there is a good deal of agreement about what the law is and how to figure it out despite deep disagreement about what makes law. It is this fact, I think, that allows so many legal practitioners and scholars to regard the debate about the nature of law with indifference. The situation would be vastly different if the two views about law led always to different conclusions about the content of the law in force.

I return to the extent to which and the ways in which disputes about the nature of law may matter in Chapter 9.

7 The Normative Force of Law

In the previous chapter, I considered the possibility that the debate over the grounds of law is a waste of time, not because it is apparently intractable, though it is, but rather because it is about something that after all doesn't matter. So long as we have theories of good governance (encompassing legitimacy, justice, and the rule of law), the ability to predict how individuals' conduct will trigger reactions from legal institutions, and theories (one for each distinct kind of legal subject) of the prudential and moral relevance of legal materials, then we have no need for an account of how to determine the content of the law in force. Though this eliminativist view is not ridiculous on its face, in the end we should not accept it. People do accept the law, in Hart's sense of treating it as a source of reasons for action, and different kinds of legal subjects (private subjects, officials of different kinds) most naturally explain the differences in the legal aspects of their practical situations in terms of their different standing with respect to the law – the different normative implications of the law for them and the different effects their decisions have on the development of the law. The distorting artificiality of trying to banish beliefs about the content of the law in force from practical deliberation is most clear when we consider the frame of mind of the lawmaker. Lawmakers do not think that they are creating legal materials that will have varying practical significance for people depending on their institutional role. They think that they are (justifiably) producing legal directives and power-conferring legal schemes that involve legitimate demands on our conduct. It is not clear that there is a coherent frame of mind available for lawmakers if they must stop thinking in this way.

But while it is true that many people are motivated to act in accordance with legal norms, it is not obvious that they ought to be; there remains the question of whether there are, in fact, prudential or moral reasons to accept the law. My focus is on the moral force of law – the ancient philosophical issue of whether there is a prima facie obligation to obey the law. The answer to this question is of obvious importance for our entire inquiry, since if there is a standing moral reason to comply with law, it evidently matters what the content of the law is.

But first, some preliminaries.

Law and Motivating Reasons

Hart's rejection of the command theory of law focused on two distinct issues. As discussed in Chapter 3, he argued that the command theory was inadequate as an account of the grounds of law because it could not explain constitutional continuity or nonimperative legal rules. But equally important for Hart was his observation that the equation of legal norms with threats made by those in power resulted in a distortion of the deliberative role law actually plays in the typical person's practical life. His main claim here is descriptive, though this isn't always clear from the exposition. It is that for most or many people, legal norms do not simply set prices on possible actions, where the price varies from context to context. We do not typically deliberate about the costs and benefits of following the law "for this case only," but accept the reason-giving force of law in general.

This descriptive observation is completely compatible with there being no general reason anybody ought to accept legal norms, and compatible with a large variety of reasons people in fact do accept them. Thus I might accept legal norms out of a sense of self-interest, moral obligation, or a mere preference to conform (Hart 1994, 203). This is the sense in which law, for Hartian positivists, can well be compared to a game. The rules of the game are what they are, and once you decide you want to play the game, there are right and wrong moves you can make; most players will be motivated to make right moves and not make wrong moves. But there is nothing in this account of the way legal rules figure in some people's deliberations that provides any reason, moral or otherwise, why anyone should play this game.

Kelsen's position here is superficially different from Hart's since, as we have also seen in Chapter 3, for Kelsen a valid legal norm is one that really does provide an "ought" and so the foundation of a legal system is, accordingly, an ought – the basic norm. In fact, however, barring quibbles over whether "validity" implies ought, and without attempting an accurate characterization of the development of Kelsen's thought over more than half a century, we can say that the two positions are identical. For Kelsen social facts determine the content of the law, but a special norm is required to animate those inert facts with obligation. That special norm has no substantive content of its own. It merely says that the norms enacted in accordance with the effective constitution ought to be obeyed. Anyone writing as a "legal scientist" can discuss the criteria of legal validity without actually accepting or "presupposing" the basic norm. The point of view of the scientist is one from which one can describe the normative system that is law *as if* the basic norm that would ground validity (obligation) were presupposed. We can make full sense of law as a normative system, a system of rules and principles, and we can note that for many people, that system is a source of motivating reasons, without having to take a stand on the further question of whether there is in fact any categorical reason anyone should pay attention to the law at all (Kelsen 1967, 201–5, 217–19; Raz 1979, 134–43).

Moral and Legal Obligation

But doesn't the positivist too assume that where there is law, obligation must be present? Hart did write that any legal theory must explain the sense in which law makes conduct "in some sense" obligatory. But by this he clearly did not mean that legal theory must explain the moral force legal norms actually have.[1] The closest he came to saying anything of the kind was when he repeatedly insisted on the opposite. That legal validity did not settle the issue of moral obligation was for Hart among the fundamental motivations of the entire positivist outlook.

Some contemporary legal philosophers do write as if positivist theory must explain how law as such can provide us with real reasons for action (e.g., Coleman 2001a, 74–102). This is puzzling, since if the content of law is grounded entirely in social fact it seems obvious that it will not always generate genuine reasons to comply. We could not have a general reason to comply with legally valid rules, just because that is what they are, no matter what their content and what the mode of their creation. More important, it is hard to see how the thought that there is always genuine reason to comply with law could ever arise if we start from the fundamental belief that law's content is grounded in social fact. The motivation for this combined view is mysterious.

What Hart had in mind when he wrote that legal theory must explain the sense in which law is a source of obligation was quite different. He believed that there was a distinct beast, a legal obligation, and that legal theory should be able to explain its existence. According to Nicola Lacey (2006, 354), Hart puzzled about the conditions for the existence of legal obligation until the end of his life. This seems to me unfortunate, since disagreement about what legal obligation is seems just as intractable as that about the grounds of law, but in the case of legal obligation nothing of importance seems to be at stake.

In his 1966 essay, "Legal Duty and Obligation," Hart (1982, 127–61) insists that the concept of legal obligation is distinct from that of moral obligation; he thus rejects the position of both Raz and Dworkin that moral obligations are the only real obligations around. Hart's position

---

[1] Shapiro (2011, 97) writes that Hart, "in all of his many writings, never explicitly explains how his positivistic theory is compatible with Hume's Law" (that you can't get an ought from an is). But Hart never suggested that you could get a genuine objective reason for action from the mere fact of legal validity.

seems on the face of it plausible; but what then is a legal obligation? There's one simple answer Hart could have given: a legal obligation is just what we have when we are subject to a valid duty-imposing legal rule. This would be to treat the idea of legal obligation as entirely internal to the system. It prompts the objection that on this account legal obligations, as such, are no more real than the obligations imposed by duties of etiquette or by the rules of a game we are playing. My own view is that a Hartian positivist should be happy to accept this result, but Hart apparently never did find it appealing.

I believe that the reason is that he was always attracted to a reductive, nonrealist account of moral obligation. If this kind of explanation is appropriate for the moral case, it is natural to provide it for the legal case as well. From this point of view, there is no normative priority to the moral; in both cases, the task is to explain the conditions under which people are inclined to say that various kinds of obligations exist. If, by contrast, we are comfortable with the idea of real, objective moral obligation or reasons for action, the important question about legal obligation is whether it implies moral obligation or not.

In *The Concept of Law*, Hart explained the existence of both moral and legal obligation in terms of his general account of social rules. "Rules are conceived and spoken of as imposing obligations when the general demand for conformity is insistent and the social pressure brought to bear upon those who deviate or threaten it is great." We then distinguish between moral and legal obligation by pointing to the involvement of certain distinctive kinds of feelings, the role of coercion, the possibility of deliberate change, and so on (1994, 82–91, 167–80). Applied to morality, Hart's account of rules and the conditions under which they generate obligation was quickly attacked by Dworkin and others, and it is one of the parts of the book that he expressly repudiated in the *Postscript*, noting that he now believed that the social rules account was appropriate only for the legal case (254–9). But this retreat was on technical grounds having to do with whether moral rules were in a certain sense conventional. Hart did not abandon his purely sociological, reductivist approach to both moral and legal obligation. His remarks make quite clear that, for both, he offers merely an account of the conditions under which it is proper to say that a certain special kind of rule exists in a society. The issue of what those with realist or objectivist commitments would think of as actual obligation is simply not confronted.[2]

It is, however, possible to take for granted an objectivist position about moral obligation and still benefit from Hart's discussion of legal obligation. Leaving aside moral obligation as a separate issue, there remains an interesting question about the difference between a legal system that is merely effective, in that its subjects generally comply, and one that is (we might say) descriptively legitimate in that there is both a demand for conformity and general acceptance of the legitimacy of that demand (Hart, 1982, 160).

If this is the right way to understand Hart, what we are left with is a dispute about the nature or concept of legal obligation. There are three contending accounts: the purely nominal account according to which legal obligation attaches to any valid duty-imposing rule, the moralized account according to which there is no legal obligation without moral obligation, and Hart's sociological account.

This, it seems clear, is a purely verbal dispute. It is plausible to restrict the idea of legal obligation to cases where there is a moral obligation, but also plausible to deny this. It is plausible to restrict the idea of legal obligation to cases where the facts fit Hart's sociological account, but also plausible not to. Suppose someone says that they have a legal obligation to turn in their dissident neighbors to the secret police. A variety of responses seems acceptable, so far as the nature or concept of legal

---

[2] Hart did not offer a purely descriptive account of moral and legal rules. For him, the normativity of moral or legal rules lies in the attitudes of those who accept those rules. This of course still does not give us objective reasons for action, as moral or legal rules will have no normative aspect for those who do not accept them. For an excellent account of Hart's metaethical views, see Raz 1993. This section discusses the cognitivist aspects of Hart's view (see Raz 1993, 148–9).

obligation is concerned. No, you have no obligation to do that, in fact it would be immoral. Yes, you have a legal obligation since the law is valid, but you have no moral reason to do it. No, you have no legal obligation because no one but the authorities would expect you to follow that legal rule. These are just different plausible ways of understanding what a legal obligation is, and I don't see any scope for so much as an argument that one of them is best.

But it doesn't matter, because we don't need the idea of legal obligation. We have the ideas of the content of the law in force and of moral obligation. That the former matters is the argument of the previous and current chapters; the latter obviously does. Hart's discussion reminds us of a third criterion that is also worth remembering: in addition to the content of valid law and moral obligation, there is the issue of the legitimacy of the law in a descriptive sense. All three issues, validity, moral obligation, and descriptive legitimacy, are important. But it is also clear that we can discuss each of them without making use of the idea of legal obligation. When claims about the conditions of legal obligation are made, it is easy enough to disambiguate, and continue the discussion using other terms. Nothing gets lost in that translation, I believe.

Authority, Legitimacy, and Political Obligation: Some Definitions

By way of stipulative definition that seems consistent with the practice of most legal philosophers, we can say that to have (real, de jure, legitimate) political *authority* is to be in a position to prescribe moral obligations for others; to have the right and the ability to do this (see, e.g., Raz 1985). It follows that there is no political authority without subjects having a general moral obligation to obey the law, and vice versa. I have always found this notion of authority to be somewhat unhelpful for political philosophy, since it seems foreign to the way actual governments and legal subjects understand their relationship, at least since the demise of the idea of the divine right of kings (see Buchanan 2007, 233–60). States do, I believe, typically claim the right to issue and enforce directives, but that leaves open whether they claim in addition that subjects have a moral obligation to obey.

In any event, our concern here is not with what states claim, but what is morally the case. There are two issues: whether the state's issuing and enforcing directives is justified, and whether subjects have a duty to obey. Some philosophers use the label "legitimacy" narrowly, to refer to the first of these issues alone; others insist that a legal system cannot count as legitimate unless both conditions are met, thus bringing the notion of legitimacy close to that of authority as defined earlier (e.g., Simmons 2001, 137). An important moral issue lies behind this terminological diversity – whether justification for a practice of directing people to act in various ways and backing that up with force can be found in the absence of a general duty to obey, and vice versa. Since my own answer to this moral question is yes, it is terminologically convenient to use "legitimacy" in the narrow sense of the moral justification of the issuing and enforcing of directives (for discussion, see Edmundson 1998, 7–47).

A related moral issue is whether subjects have some kind of general duty to support the institutions that constitute the state. This issue is most naturally labeled one of "political obligation," and so that is the terminology I use. (Here again there is terminological diversity, however, as for many writers "political obligation" refers to the obligation to obey the law.) I do not in this book pretend to address the issues of legitimacy or political obligation for their own sakes, but only as they are implicated in different views one might have about the duty to obey the law.

The Duty to Obey and the Theory of Law

The issue of whether there is an obligation to obey the law interacts directly with the issue of the grounds of law, which poses an initial problem.

Dworkin approaches the theory of the grounds of law with the premise that legal rights and obligations are, generally speaking, real – that is, objective, moral – rights and obligations. On this approach, the question of whether a norm is plausibly regarded as having moral force is part of the inquiry into whether it is a legal norm in the first place. Positivism doesn't assume that law is not morally significant; but it does insist that a belief that it is morally significant cannot govern our investigation into its content.[3] This is true even for Raz, as although in his view law claims that it gives us genuine obligations to obey, he does not hold that we should interpret law so that this claim is more likely to come out true. In fact, he argues that the claim is usually false, though there is plenty of valid law around (Raz 1979, 233–49; 1994, 325–38).

Kelsen, as we have seen, did hold that insofar as the *Grundnorm* was presupposed, law was genuinely normative. There is an interesting scholarly debate to be had about just what he meant by presupposition of a norm, and about just what legal normativity implied for him. As discussed in Chapter 3, it is possible to read him as equating legal normativity, where it exists, with the normativity of morality and justice, but also possible to read him as insisting, in line with the purity of the pure theory, that they must be distinct. For current purposes, however, there is no need to enter into the debate about how best to read Kelsen on normativity. Suppose that he believed that law is a source of oughts distinct from morality (and self-interested rationality). We can leave such a view to one side. The idea of a distinct realm of categorical reasons for action, emerging from legal practices, is both mysterious and implausible. If law gives rise to real obligations, they are going to be moral obligations. If we suppose, on the other hand, that Kelsen believed that legal oughts were not some different species than moral oughts, we have different grounds for not pursuing his position. For whatever else may be said about Kelsen's views and their development, it is crucial to take account of his lifelong rejection of moral objectivity. Like Hart, Kelsen simply did not offer a view on the relation between valid law and objective moral obligation.[4]

---

[3] Such a stance is also compatible with nonpositivist theories of the grounds of law, just not Dworkin's.

[4] Kelsen's moral subjectivism no doubt considerably weakened his ability to defend the constitutional order of the Weimar Republic against critics (Dyzenhaus 1997, 158–60).

Most discussions of the obligation to obey the law in moral and political philosophy implicitly assume a positivist position. These discussions
take for granted that law can have any content and be created by all kinds
of regimes, democratic or despotic. So it is hardly a surprise (the nonpositivist might quietly observe) that the conclusion of these inquiries is
usually that there is no general duty to obey the law.

It would seem, then, that we cannot discuss the question of the duty
to obey without at the same time taking a stand on the grounds of law
(Soper 2002). This would be unfortunate, since the normative force of
law, if such there is, would be one main reason to inquire into its grounds
in the first place. However, this problem can be avoided if we confine
our discussion to the area of overlap among plausible accounts of the
grounds of law described in the previous chapter. As we saw, positivist
and nonpositivist accounts agree in very many cases about the factors
relevant to determining the content of law. When discussing the duty to
obey, we should have in mind not the death penalty, same-sex marriage,
and the regulation of sexual conduct among consenting adults, but rather
road rules, duties of care, formation doctrine in contract law, the law of
theft, and the like.

Since the traditional question is whether there is a duty to obey law
as such – just because it is the law and not because of its content or even,
perhaps, the way it was made – it can be objected that this narrowing
of focus to only some of what on some theories counts as law makes it
impossible to provide an answer. But in fact it only makes it impossible
to defend a positive answer. If there is no content-independent prima
facie duty to obey the law that falls into the overlap, then there is no
content-independent prima facie duty to obey the law. This will be my
conclusion.

But it does save his theory from absurdity. It is obviously not plausible, morally speaking, to claim that whatever the rules established in accordance with the effective constitution may be, they impose objective moral obligations. If legal validity implies real
obligation, legally valid rules couldn't have any old content and be posited in any
old way.

A more particular objection is that there cannot be *any* overlap in the implications of a theory of law like Dworkin's that assumes that there is a general duty to obey and those of theories that leave that issue open.[5] My argument in the previous chapter that positivist and nonpositivist theories will in many cases agree about the factors that are relevant to answering some legal question ignored this issue. Nonpositivism is just the view that moral considerations always play a role in fixing the content of law. But once we add to nonpositivism the distinctive claim that legal duties are in their nature real moral duties, do we still find an overlap with positivist theories? It might be thought that we could not, since for Dworkinian nonpositivism the status of answers to legal questions is categorically different than for positivist approaches. For Dworkinians, the question of whether there is a general duty to comply with legal directives is empty. So mustn't I have left this particular version of nonpositivism aside when I inquire into the normative force of what falls into the overlap?

I do not think so. A theory of the grounds of law cannot simply announce that legal rights and obligations are real (moral) rights and obligations. That does not help us determine the content of the law. What we need is an account, such as Dworkin's interpretivist moral reading, that tells us how we figure out what the law is. That account may itself have been shaped in part by the interpretive assumption that legal rights and obligations are real rights and obligations, and so the content of the moral reading will turn in part on a certain theory about the duty to obey – in Dworkin's case the theory of associative obligations, discussed later in this chapter. But this does not mean that we cannot say what the law is according to this account unless we accept the theory of the duty to obey. Once we have determined the area of overlap, we can ask whether the account of the duty to obey that partly shaped the interpretivist moral reading really does establish a general duty to obey.

---

[5] I thank George Letsas, Stefan Sciaraffa, and Nicos Stavropoulos for pressing me on this.

The Duty to Obey – Individuals

Our question is whether there is a prima facie duty to obey the law. A prima facie duty is one that could be overridden in particular cases by other factors of sufficient moral weight. I am not aware of any argument for an absolute or non-overridable duty to obey the law, whatever its content may be. And by a duty to obey the law, we mean a duty to obey the law *as such*, because it is the law, and not because of its content or the way it was made (Green 1988, 225–6).

I have nothing new to say about the most familiar deontological argument for a duty to obey the law, Locke's argument of actual contract, or consent. Both elements of Hume's argument against this account in the *Treatise of Human Nature* and "Of the Original Contract" are convincing. Suppose that I have promised to obey the law, perhaps when I became a naturalized citizen of my adopted country.[6] Though I cannot argue the case here, I agree with Hume that the duty to keep promises is itself instrumentally grounded – I should keep promises made primarily because of the value of the practice of doing so, though other moral factors are relevant when the promise is not made to a stranger. But if that is so, there is every reason to look directly to the instrumental case for obeying the law – the good that a practice of general obedience generally brings about. It is true that if I have promised to obey, there are other instrumental benefits to add to the mix, but on the face of it they seem swamped by the direct benefits of obedience.

The second part of Hume's argument is that most individual legal subjects have not in any case promised to obey the law; they were born into a society where obedience is simply expected of them. Tacit consent,

---

[6] It is worth pointing out that the Oath of Naturalization of the United States does not include such a promise. It does include these words: "that I will support and defend the Constitution and laws of the United States of America against all enemies, foreign and domestic; that I will bear true faith and allegiance to the same." But all that is compatible with civil disobedience, at least of the kind Martin Luther King, Jr. advocated in "Letter from Birmingham Jail."

inferred from continuing presence in the jurisdiction, is implausible because most people have no realistic alternative.

The argument of "fair play" is subject to a similarly well-known and compelling objection. This argument is based on the plausible idea that if I have chosen to share in the benefits of a cooperative scheme, it would be morally objectionable to free ride on the burdensome compliance of others by not shouldering the burdens of compliance myself. But most individuals cannot be said to have chosen to participate in the cooperative scheme that is governance by law. And when benefits are forced on one, the fair play argument does not have any purchase (Nozick 1974, 90–5).

Quite apart from that familiar objection, however, it cannot simply be assumed that following the law amounts to assuming the burdens of cooperation in the sense relevant for the fair play argument (Greenawalt 1989, 138–47; Raz 1979, 237–9). There certainly can be valid legal requirements, such as some pointless bureaucratic requirement, the universal flouting of which would not reduce the benefits people receive from the overall legal scheme or otherwise undermine it. Even if every legal subject had asked for the benefits of the legal system, the argument from fair play would not support a fully general duty to obey the law. It would support a duty to shoulder one's share of the burdens of sustaining the beneficial scheme; but that is not the same thing.

I believe a similar point applies to Dworkin's (1986, 195–215) argument that a prima facie duty to obey the law can be grounded in associative obligations.[7] Dworkin's key idea is that law can transform a group of people living together by "geographical accident" into what he calls a political community. The members of a political community, in his special sense, bear associative obligations to each other akin to those held among members of a family. Law creates this political fraternity by providing a

---

[7] This account will not ground an entirely content- and context-independent duty to obey unless we presuppose Dworkin's theory of law, according to which the various conditions for the existence of an associative obligation are guaranteed to be satisfied by valid law, since the content of law will be determined with those conditions in mind as constraints.

moral bond in the form of moral principles that are shared, despite disagreement about ideals of justice and sound policy.

We may accept for the sake of argument that where members of a group share principles to govern their interaction despite their moral disagreements at the level of ideal theory, their relationship acquires a special moral quality such that they owe obligations to each other that they do not owe to outsiders. We may also accept that the content of that obligation is to be true to the shared principles that constitute the community in the first place. Even if we grant all this, however, it does not follow that there is a general obligation to obey the law, because there is no reason to think that all and only the principles we share will be expressed in the law (Murphy 2001a, 397–409). We do not simply enact into law our shared moral values or commitments; we enact into law rules, principles, and standards that are appropriately enacted into law, given our shared values and commitments, and given the special considerations that have to be taken into account when we are making law, not expressing our values and commitments. To take a simple example, the Anglo-Saxon world surely shares a commitment to a moral principle of easy rescue. Yet, rightly or wrongly, Anglo-Saxon lawmakers have generally felt that it would be inappropriate to give that principle legal expression (Murphy 2001b). Similarly, there are good reasons why the reach of contract law should not extend to all promises that (as we agree) have moral force.

But even though not all principles we share have appropriate legal expression, wouldn't fidelity to a community of principle nonetheless *include* fidelity to those principles that do get expressed in the law? No, because legal principles may not merely fall short of shared moral principles, they may, on their surface, mislead in a more fundamental way. It would be wrong, for example, to conclude from the law of property and its related doctrines in torts and criminal law that underlying that whole scheme is some shared commitment to a Lockean theory of moral property rights.[8] Whatever one thinks about this one example, it cannot

---

[8] See the discussion of "everyday libertarianism" in Murphy and Nagel (2002, 31–7).

be denied that much of the content of law does not wear its rationale on its face. Legal principles do not all simply announce moral principles with the same content; many of them are part of an artificial normative scheme whose justification must be found elsewhere. And from the fact that some shared value is served instrumentally by enacting some principle into law, it does not follow that that value is best promoted by each individual being faithful to that legal principle in every case.

If we are to have general moral reason to follow legal rules, the most promising source may seem to be the process of their making. Many have thought that democratically enacted legislation does bring with it a standing duty of compliance because of the moral significance of the procedure. Any argument along these lines is limited, of course, both to the case of (good enough) democracies and to legislation. But in any case, it seems to me that the argument does not go through. Consider, for example, Thomas Christiano's suggestion that to fail to abide by democratic legislative directives is to treat one's fellow citizens unequally and thus unjustly. "Citizens who skirt democratically made law act contrary to the equal right of all citizens to have a say in making laws when there is substantial and informed disagreement" (2008, 250). There is serious ground for doubt whether actually existing democracies respect an equal right of all citizens to have a say in making laws. But we can leave that aside, and grant that an ideal democracy satisfies the equal right of citizens to have a say in making laws and is for that reason (if not for that reason alone) a superior mode of lawmaking. Other forms of lawmaking, we may say, violate this equal right. What is unclear is why an individual's failure to obey democratically made law also violates the right.

Assume an ideal electoral and legislative process that respects the equal right of all to have a say in making laws. When I disobey the law that results, I am not asserting that the democratic process was not the right way to make law, nor that I have the right to tell others what to do, or even to make a special exception for myself. The moral reasons for adopting a particular process of lawmaking are not automatically grounds for obedience, unless we simply assume that we have an obligation to obey law made in the right way.

We cannot assimilate democratic lawmaking to cases where groups of people agree to adopt a certain procedure, regarded as fair, for resolving their disagreement. Suppose two of us have to paint the house, but both prefer to use the roller to paint the walls and ceiling than the brush to paint the woodwork. We agree to draw straws. We should comply with the outcome of the chosen procedure; but this is because we agreed in advance to do just that. The case of democratic governance is different from this simple case in two ways. First, I might agree to or support a method for making law without this entailing an agreement or promise to obey. Second, as is obvious, democratic procedures are not based on universal agreement; they are imposed on the population, independent of actual consent. Even if some degree of actual support among the population – legitimacy in the descriptive sense – is treated as a condition of normative legitimacy, unanimous support is clearly unavailable.

In some cases, it seems that we ought to follow the decision made in a fair procedure, even if there was no advance agreement to do that. When the members of a group have agreed that some collective task will be performed by them, but disagree about the division of labor, it may seem unnecessary that each agree in advance to follow the results of a particular fair procedure. While each of us is grumbling that he does not want to go first, one of the group may draw my name out of a hat. Assuming we are all equally well suited to going first, there's no better procedure than that. So I should go first even though I didn't in any sense agree to the procedure in advance. But again, democratic government is not a bit like this, because we have not agreed in advance on a certain list of collective tasks that require a certain division of labor.

Christiano well expresses what seems to me to be a widely held view. I have so far been suggesting that its apparent appeal is due to a tacit association of democracy with some kind of universal consent. But perhaps what is at work is rather an idea that we are all morally required to do our part in the collective enterprise of promoting and maintaining valuable and just forms of social cooperation (see Finnis 1980, 1984). Democracy presents itself as the morally best means of resolving disagreements about how to go about that and should be supported for that reason, independent of any actual consent to anything. This seems an attractive view, but it still does not get us to a general duty to obey the law. We should obey the law, on this essentially instrumental line of thought, just in case that will further our duty to promote whatever social goals justify the existence of the (legitimate) coercive political apparatus in the first place. As discussed more fully later, we cannot simply stipulate that compliance with law will always have this effect.

Other defenses of democracy as a system of government, such those that turn on the epistemic value of democratic procedures, or on the value of public deliberation, will, it seems evident, leave the same gap between justification of the system of government and the obligation to obey the law. (Jürgen Habermas's [1996] account of the justification of any norm, legal or moral, closes the gap at the level of ideal theory, insofar as justification can only be found where certain ideal procedures have in fact been followed. But this does not imply a general duty to obey law under actual, nonideal conditions.)

All the arguments so far considered for a content- and context-independent duty to obey the law have a similar structure. They are all compatible with or explicitly invoke an instrumental understanding of the moral reasons in favor of governance by law as an institution; the attempt is then made to provide a deontological, or noninstrumental, account of the duty to obey.

Now by an instrumental understanding I mean that governance by law is valued in the first place because of its ability to secure certain good outcomes. Were it not for the value of those outcomes, we would not regard governance by law as morally desirable; law is not valuable just for its own sake. This position is of course compatible with legal governance being morally superior to other means of promoting security, overall welfare, justice, and so on, even if the other forms of governance could do a better job promoting such ends. Law as a means has noninstrumental virtues; there may, in fact, be no other fully morally acceptable means available for the promotion of these social goals. So the instrumental view of law is fully compatible with valuing law as one mode of governance among others because it can satisfy the values we associate with the ideal of the rule of law (see also Green 2010). It is also compatible with there being moral principles that apply only to the legal order, as part of what Rawls (1996, 257–88) calls the basic structure of society, and not directly to individuals. Thus some goals of legal governance, such as social justice, may make no sense independently of the existence of some institutional governance structures. What is ruled out by an instrumental view of law is that governance by law has some kind of intrinsic moral significance that it would have even if it contributed not at all to security, justice, higher levels of overall welfare, and the rest. On the instrumental view, though there are moral reasons to favor governance by law over other forms of governance, no form of governance, governance by law included, would have value for us if it did not bring about independent goods. The instrumental view of law is therefore compatible with the Utopian Marxist ideal of the withering away of the state.

A noninstrumental account of the value of governance by law could in principle provide a more direct route to the conclusion that there is a standing moral reason to obey the law. But I am not aware of any such account – at least not one that applies in the actual, nonideal world.

Kant's legal theory perhaps comes closest, since for Kant positive law plays a constitutive role, making real all "acquired" rights and specifying, for the situation where people are subject to a coercive power, the content of the one "innate" right to equal freedom (Kant 1996; for discussion see Ripstein 2009). Moreover, though there are grounds for criticism of the content of these rights as actually found in positive law, no individual is in a position to act on his view that the state has got it wrong. This suggests that positive law in some sense constitutes (some of what is) right and wrong. It also suggests that Kant's view that we have a duty to enter into the "rightful condition" that is life under a state should be understood in terms of the intrinsic moral value of being governed by law. It isn't that we need law because that is the best way to protect everyone's independently cognizable rights; it is that without law it is in some sense impossible for us to act rightly toward each other. Without law we are doomed to a life of sin; where there is law, we must always comply.

But now even if governance by law is necessary for the realization of the equal right to freedom (Ripstein 2009, 9), that does not make being subject to public authority an end in itself. Second, while Kant does assert that we must all "obey the authority who has power over you" he immediately adds "in whatever does not conflict with inner morality" (1996, 136). The important point here is that Kant's doctrine of right is concerned with the grounds for the use of force. So it does not address in any great detail the general moral significance of governance by law, nor in particular the question of when and whether passive noncompliance with law is morally permissible (Hill 2002).

So far as I can see, the instrumental view of law as I have laid it out is inescapable. There is of course nothing inconsistent in offering a deontological account of the duty to obey the directives of a system whose existence is at bottom justified in instrumental terms, and no way to prove that it could not work. Notably, the consent argument has the right form for this kind of approach. The consent argument is unlike the other arguments considered previously in that it doesn't leave a gap between the justification of the system and the conclusion of a general duty to obey. But this is because the consent argument applies entirely independently of the justification and indeed the quality of the system of governance by law – everything turns on the content of the contractual arrangement between subject and ruler with limits set only by considerations of contractual capacity and the absence of force and fraud. The argument applies directly to each subject but is entirely detached from the reasons anyone may have for valuing a situation of governance by law. In fact, once we leave aside the idea that governance by law has intrinsic moral significance for each subject, it is tempting to speculate that the only deontological argument that could in principle ground a general duty to obey is a voluntaristic one such as the argument

from consent.[9] (The argument from consent is not the only possible voluntaristic argument. Thus Raz's [1979, 250–61; 1994, 337–8] idea that
those who "identify" with or respect their legal system may acquire a
duty to obey is voluntaristic, even though there is no relevant canonical
moment akin to the making of a promise.)

Even if there are deontological reasons to favor certain forms of legal
order over others – those that respect the autonomy of subjects, or the
value of integrity, or are democratic, and so on – a further argument is
required to link each legal directive to each subject's obligations. Take the
morally best, humanly feasible legal and political system we can describe.
Why should each subject always obey each law? Only, I suspect, if each of
us has taken some voluntary step to bind us morally to all of the law.[10]

[9] I here echo much of what Simmons (1979, 2001, 2005) writes about the duty to obey
the law. But with Greenawalt (1989, 167), I disagree with Simmons that an account of
the duty to obey the law must explain why we have special obligations to obey the
law of one state (our own) in particular. Simmons's motivation for this "particularity
requirement" is not one that applies to my discussion: it is to challenge claims of legitimacy by the state, which he holds can only be made good if all citizens have a partic-
ularized moral obligation to obey. (It is worth noting that even the consent argument,
which Simmons agrees is the only hope for a general duty to obey, could violate the
particularity requirement, in that it is certainly possible to promise obedience to more
than one state.) As I am here simply investigating what moral obligation we have to
obey the law, there is no reason to insist in advance that our conclusion will have a certain content. In any event, an instrumental account of political obligation of the kind
about to be discussed could certainly impose on individuals stronger responsibility
for maintaining the institutions of states to which they have closer ties. Furthermore,
even if I have a fully impersonal responsibility to promote just and beneficial institutions wherever they may be, the relevance of my compliance with law to fulfilling that
responsibility will generally be restricted to law that claims jurisdiction over me, which
is for the most part the law of my current country of residence. For discussion of these
issues, see Waldron 1999. (The formal legal category of citizenship, naturalization oaths
aside, is not especially relevant to the issue of the duty to obey. Think of the Palestinian
citizen of Jordan who has lived all his life in Lebanon, or the Australian or Mexican
citizen who has lived most of his life in the United States.)

[10] Stephen Perry (2013) has recently suggested the following account of political authority, which would, if its elements were substantively made out, ground a general duty:
a lawmaker has the power to give others obligations just in case it would be good if it
had that power. This is related to Anscombe's (1990) idea that the state has authority
because it is necessary that it does; but Perry, unlike Anscombe, explicitly focuses in

Of course, if law as such has instrumental importance, we would expect there to be instrumental reasons people should at least sometimes obey the law. Those who offer deontological arguments for a duty to obey need not and do not disagree about that. But the argument thus far suggests that the only moral reasons to obey the law are instrumental. And with that foundation, it is clear that we cannot build a content- and context-independent duty for individuals to obey.

The moral reason to obey the law is that it will do (if it will) more good than not obeying. For individuals, the good that it may do is that it will support the institutions of the state and promote what, through law, the state is trying to achieve. The instrumental duty to obey the law is thus subsidiary to an instrumental duty of political obligation. This is the position not just of the utilitarian tradition that follows Hume, but also of Rawls (1999, 99), who characterizes political obligation in terms of a natural duty of justice – to support and promote just institutions. Rawls's account of political obligation is clearly consequentialist, or instrumental, though it is of course not utilitarian. (Rawls [308] does, however, write: "There is quite clearly no difficulty in explaining why we are to comply with just laws enacted under a just constitution." It is quite unclear to me how the instrumental natural duty of justice could do any such thing.)

There are clear benefits to the existence of institutions that can provide basic security, protect rights, preserve the environment, promote economic justice and overall welfare, and so on. And law as a mode of

on what would explain the state's having the power to impose obligations on others as distinct from the good that the exercise of coercive force might do. Even leaving behind the puzzling form of this argument (it would be good, therefore it is), it is entirely unclear why there would *ever* be value in X having such a power with respect to Y. It might be good for subjects to believe that they have a duty to do what the government says; but why, independently of any effect on conduct, would the mere fact of the moral relationship – I get to tell you what you ought to do – have value? Even if the state is democratic, and so the duties are imposed after a fair process that treats us all equally, and so on, there still seems no plausible case that it would be good in itself for the state to have this "normative power." The case is different from that of promising, where it is at least arguable that there is value in my being able to tie myself to you by way of promissory obligation. On these issues, see Edmundson (2010).

governance is clearly superior to alternatives, from the moral point of view, in view of its potential to achieve such goals while at the same time respecting the agency of persons. There may be law without the rule of law, but only legal systems can achieve the ideal of the rule of law, which is the best way to rule. All this is obvious enough as a matter of political theory, even abstracting from debates about what exactly the conditions for a legitimate coercive political order are, and what account of justice we should be aspiring to.

Suppose a context where the political coercive order is legitimate and otherwise good enough so that revolution and overthrow is morally a worse option than supporting, while trying to improve, the content of the law, the context of its making, and the mode of its enforcement. On the instrumental account, it is clear that we subjects have, by way of political obligation, a duty not to undermine but rather to support the existing order. The issue then becomes whether this implies that we also have a duty to obey the law. And the answer, of course, is that it depends. It depends on whether we do more good – in terms of our twin aims of supporting the existing order and making things better – by complying or by not complying.

The basic structural point is this, and it applies even if the law is as good as it could be. We cannot reason directly from what it would be good and right to have enacted and enforced as law to what it would be good or right for individuals to do (see Edmundson 1998, 7–47). That we have the law in place that it is best to enforce (there is no better set of legal norms it would be better to enforce) does not imply that it is always obligatory for each person to follow the law. Of course, so long as the continued existence of the legal system is desirable, it pretty much follows that it would be bad if *everyone* disobeyed *all* the laws, since the consequence of everyone disobeying all the time, most likely, would be collapse of the system. But even disobedience by all might not undermine the overall structure, so long as it is restricted to certain parts of the legal order. Thus suppose we believe that the prohibition of recreational use of marijuana, or a requirement that undocumented persons be reported to the Department of Homeland Security, would be bad policy. Suppose also pretty much everyone fails to comply. The state will not collapse. It might actually improve, in terms of the content of its law.

There is a puzzle about the case of general disobedience, of all law, that needs to be mentioned and then set aside. If no one complies, the (good enough) state falls, which, we presume, is a bad result. But it seems as if no one of us is to blame. Suppose general compliance; my becoming a noncomplier won't cause the state to fall. Suppose general noncompliance; my having stayed a complier wouldn't have saved the state. It is tempting to reason that no instrumental account can ever show why any individual ought to obey the law. But this temptation has its roots in a very general phenomenon – if we submit to it, we will conclude that no trivial act of pollution is bad because of its effects, no failure to vote is bad because of its effects, no failure to contribute money to famine relief is bad because of its effects, and so on. The general problem is how to explain individual responsibility in a context where, as Derek Parfit (1984, 75–86) puts it, "we together" cause some harm. It is a fascinating and important philosophical puzzle, but its generality allows me to leave it aside here.

Suppose I know that enough others are complying such that my non-complying act would not be part of a group of acts that together have a bad effect on the viability of the legal system.[11] If I reason that my non-compliance won't make any difference, could I be said to be free riding on the compliance of others?[12] This is not the argument from fair play. The

---

[11] Exactly how to determine whether my act should count as part of such a group is an important part of the general puzzle about collective responsibility for bad outcomes. Obviously, the test cannot be whether, taken on its own, my act makes a difference. But neither should we say that all acts of the type that together make a difference are part of the group, since it may make no difference if there are many fewer complying acts. There is going to have to be some account of a vague boundary here. As I say, pursuing this important issue here would take us too far afield.

[12] Wellman (2005, 30–53) discusses this issue in the context of advancing an argument that the duty to obey the law arises out of a duty to rescue; for effective criticism of Wellman's "Samaritanism" argument, see Simmons (2005, 179–88); Edmundson (2004, 249–52).

thought is that if we together have an obligation to act so as to preserve the state, because of what it can achieve, it is unfair of any one person to count on sufficient compliance by others, taking any advantage that might result from his own noncompliance. "You only get not to comply because we are complying," say the compliers to the noncompliers, "and that's not fair." "If we could count on you to comply, it would be all right for us not to comply." This seems right, but the issue is rarely going to come up in a pure way. For most people most of the time, self-interest counsels compliance, in which case the compliance of the compliers is not a sacrifice or burden for them. Equally, the reason for noncompliance might not be my own advantage as there may be none; in that case too there would be no free riding. In principle, then, a deontological requirement of fairness to complying others is fully compatible with the instrumental case for compliance. The circumstances of its engagement, however, are rather particular, and perhaps typically not present.

Suppose then that the level of compliance is sufficient to assure the stability of the state and the circumstances do not raise the fairness issue just discussed. If we now consider the case of an individual who is debating whether to comply with a legal rule, it is easy to see that the mere fact that it is a legal rule is likely to provide only very weak grounds for compliance. No one act of noncompliance will in itself bring the whole scheme down – not in virtue of its own effects, nor in virtue of the "bad example" it might provide. It may be that in this particular context, for this particular individual, following it may actually achieve little or nothing in the way of the benefits we associate with general compliance.

Now in the case of some very particular legal rules, individual acts of noncompliance can directly harm the overall institutional regime that is governance by law. I have in mind legal rules prohibiting the corrupting, through bribery or otherwise, of legal officials – judges, policemen, legislators, and so on.[13] In this case, the harm to the overall system is not dependent on the overall level of compliance.

---

[13] I am grateful here to Leslie Green.

Equally, there often will be moral reasons to act in accordance with a legal rule that are not related to the benefits of maintaining a legal order. Thus suppose some scheme of environmental regulation establishes a fair cooperative scheme that has effective results in cleaning up some river (see Raz 1979). Even total noncompliance with this scheme would not endanger the legal order. But each potential polluter has instrumental moral reasons, supplemented by reasons of fairness, to participate in the scheme. These reasons, however, are content dependent; they are not guaranteed to be present just because the scheme is put in place by law. Furthermore, and needless to say, there are direct moral reasons to refrain from most of what is prohibited by the criminal law.

All in all, we have to conclude that for individuals in a well-functioning state, the instrumental moral case to comply with the law just because it is the law is rather weak, and in any event hostage to all kinds of contingencies. What seems to matter much more than the obedience of individual subjects is their seeking reform of the state and the content of its laws to make it more legitimate, more just, and all around better. In a more or less effective state, where effective coercive measures in any event provide adequate reasons of self-interest for most people to obey most of the time, the moral case for compliance with law just doesn't seem to be very strong.

The Law-Abiding Character

There is a further important aspect to the issue, however. We have considered the morality of compliance only as a question of what it is right or wrong to do. We have not evaluated the case for what Hume called the artificial virtue of political allegiance.[14]

Hume's moral theory focused solely on virtues of character, the motives and dispositions that receive moral approval or disapproval. He

---

[14] Thanks to Thomas Nagel for discussion. For exploration of the idea that "law-abidance" might be a virtue in the classical, noninstrumental sense, see Edmundson 2006.

argued that some such motives and dispositions, such as parental love, are found in nature. Others, such as law abidingness and fidelity to promise, can only arise in the context of a conventional social practice and are therefore properly regarded as artificial. Hume believed that a standing disposition to comply with law would in the first instance be generated by self-interest; moral approval by others, on the other hand, is grounded in the recognition that this disposition has social utility. Now neither Hume's exclusive focus on virtue in his moral theory nor his claim that self-interest is the original ground of the virtue of compliance is essential to the structure of his argument. Instrumentalist moral theory generally should recognize value in dispositions and motives that themselves can be seen to make things go better.

That consequentialist moral theory should evaluate not just conduct but also character was most clearly argued by Sidgwick (1982). More recently, philosophers have appealed to this plurality of objects of evaluation to defend consequentialism against the charge that it (absurdly) requires strict impartiality at the level of disposition, motive, and desire (Parfit 1984, 3–51; Railton 1984). These discussions show, in effect, that consequentialist ethical theory can explain the moral significance of the natural virtues.

The same general approach can be applied to Humean artificial virtues. An instrumental theory of the duty to comply should consider not just the reasons we may have to act in compliance with law; it should also consider the instrumental value of subjects having a general disposition toward compliance. If we have such a disposition, we typically don't reflect on the reasons for compliance, but simply act. But the disposition need not and should not be blind habit. When called on to reflect on such dispositions, we can justify them as tending to promote good outcomes. Since we are able to offer justificatory reasons for our standing policy of compliance, this complex of beliefs and motives is entirely compatible with Hart's account of what it is to accept the law, and the internal aspect of legal rules.

The question now becomes whether it is instrumentally for the best for legal subjects to have a standing disposition to comply. The importance of this possibility lies in the fact that the disposition might be for the best even if in some cases compliance is not for the best. Taking into account the possibility of error, especially a tendency to err in our own favor, we may do better, overall and in the long run of cases, not considering the merits of acting in a certain way on a case-by-case basis, but simply sticking to a firm policy. These points have been made by utilitarians attempting to answer deontological critics (Hare 1982). Yes, say the utilitarians, you should adopt a policy of never killing innocent people, even though on some occasions that will mean you do the wrong thing. You reconsider the grounds for your policy only when the circumstances are truly exceptional. If you fail to kill when the circumstances were not such as to justify reviewing the policy, but killing would have nonetheless been for the best, you will have done the wrong thing, though your motive not to kill was a good one. We might say that your failure to kill was blamelessly wrong (Parfit 1984, 31–5), since you acted on a motive it was right for you to have. This is not a compelling answer to the deontological critic, since the judgment that refraining from killing the innocent was wrong should be rejected. But in the context of the duty to obey, where deontological arguments for compliance are not plausible, the idea of it being right to adopt a standing policy to act in a way that will on occasion lead us to act less well than we otherwise might is clearly very important.

Nonetheless, it does not seem to be true that for individuals acting in their private capacity it is generally for the best to be disposed to comply with law without considering the pros and cons of the particular case. Law has varying content, and we are adept at sorting legal rules into relevant different categories without much thought. I can distinguish between legal rules prohibiting recreational use of marijuana, say, and rules of tax law. Most important, it is not difficult for us to identify cases where overall compliance with law can be counted on, so that my noncompliance won't harm the legal-political institutional order, from cases where that is not so. Thus though it may in some circumstances, and for some categories of legal rules, be for the best to develop a standing disposition to comply, there is no compelling reason to think that a disposition always to comply with law as such will be for the best.

It is true, as I argued in the previous chapter, that we cannot rephrase people's acceptance of law in other terms. We have also seen that we should have an expansive understanding of what acceptance amounts to, one that includes motives and dispositions and not just beliefs. It nonetheless still appears that the moral case for accepting the law is rather weak. If that is so, one still may wonder just how important this entire inquiry into the determinants of the content of law really is.

The Duty of States to Obey the Law

Everything changes when we turn to the law that applies to the state itself. Here we cannot restrict our focus primarily to the content of law and the mode of its making, assuming more or less effective (and legitimate) enforcement. There is no further set of institutions that will enforce the law that applies to states themselves. Once again, I focus here on domestic law, leaving international law to the next chapter.

Though it is obvious, it is also often forgotten that there is no coercive apparatus that will enforce law against the government itself. In countries such as the United States or Germany, the institution of judicial review may blind us to this, since for justiciable constitutional and statutory questions the court is there to pronounce that some legislation is invalid or some executive act was contrary to law. But pronouncement, obviously, is not enforcement (Goldsmith & Levinson 2009). Enforcement of law happens when the executive branch of government uses coercive means to ensure compliance by individual subjects of the state. When a highest court finds executive or legislative illegality, we rely on the relevant branches simply to comply. Of course, the executive branch may enforce the law against lower-level officials of that branch. But if the executive branch as a whole is not complying – in practice, if the highest-level officials are not complying – there is no further enforcement mechanism available. (I leave aside the possible case of high-level members of the executive branch being prosecuted by a later government for violation of the criminal law. Apart from the fact that such prosecution rarely if ever happens, in situations of stable democratic transition at any rate, the issue of government compliance is obviously not limited to the criminal law.)

A related issue here, discussed more fully in the next chapter, is the idea that coercive enforcement is a condition of the existence of law. Most legal philosophers now reject the thought that sanctions must be present before we can talk sensibly of legal order. But few emphasize that if we took that view, we would have to conclude not only that states are not subject to international law, but that they are not subject to law at all (for an exception, see Raz 1999, 158). Though, as I argue in the next chapter, it would be wrong to deny the importance of the possibility of coercion when distinguishing law from other normative systems, it is disastrous to insist that the presence of an actual coercive apparatus is a requirement for the existence of legal norms. That would lead us in exactly the wrong direction, away from the domain in which law has its greatest normative significance.

What moral reasons do legal officials in the executive, judicial, and legislative branches have to follow constitutional and ordinary domestic law? I should first mention and set aside the unlawful use of coercive force by the executive branch against its subjects.[15] Though I do not here attempt to offer a theory of legitimacy, it does seem plausible that any justification for the use of force that might attach to the state in virtue of its existence as the publically constituted coercive order (as opposed merely to being in a position to do something) will depend on the existence of law and the state's compliance with it. As I suggested previously, though law and legal institutions would have no moral significance if they could do no good, governance by and through law may be an essential condition of any legitimate coercive pursuit of those aims.

But the issue of official compliance is much broader than this specific case of unlawful coercion of subjects. What general moral reasons do

---

[15] I am grateful here to Alexander Guerrero.

legal officials have to comply with law? They may have promised to do so, either by an explicit oath, or perhaps by an implicit promise that can be inferred from their action in accepting office or seeking it through the electoral process. This will not necessarily apply to all legal officials, in all kinds of legal orders. But even where there is an express promise, I do not believe, for the reasons given earlier, that this can provide a quick foundation for the duty to obey. Even if some deontological account of the morality of promise were available, it should still be clear that the really weighty reasons legal officials should obey lie elsewhere.

The main reason legal officials should obey the law is again instrumental. U.S. constitutional electoral law has some glaring imperfections, such as the Electoral College, the overrepresentation of residents of low-population states in the Senate, and the ridiculously short electoral term for the House of Representatives. Wouldn't it be good if somehow the relevant officials could conspire simply to change the practice, without amending the law? It would be in one way good, but in another way extremely bad. When it comes to individuals, the "bad example" claim about noncompliance seems silly. When it comes to government officials setting examples for each other, and for the rest of us, it does not. Moreover, and more important, the very idea of the state being subject to law being taken seriously depends on states taking that idea seriously. Once the decision whether to comply starts to be treated as a matter of deciding whether there is a better way to do things, we quickly end up with the state not binding itself to law at all. The benefits of the constitutional state, in terms of continuity, stability, transparency, the avoidance of usurpation, and so on, depend on close to full compliance with law by the state itself.[16]

The importance of the various branches of government following the law is not limited to the structural parts of a constitution, or even

---

[16] In their argument that the executive branch of the United States is not bound by law and it's a good thing too, Posner and Vermeule (2011) simply assume that the basic constitutional framework of the state will remain in place.

to constitutional law itself. Suppose that the executive branch of some government deliberately flouts a statute requiring legislative authorization for the use of military force. There are obvious weighty moral reasons (quick action my save lives) that would support this in a particular case, as well as, on the other hand, standing moral reasons in favor of broader public deliberation about the decision to risk lives in military action. It might seem that the additional moral reasons generated by a legal prohibition could not possibly have comparable weight. But the bad effects of official lawlessness are of a fundamentally different order of magnitude from those of individual noncompliance. And the effects are more severe, the higher up the political hierarchy you go. If the head of government flouts the law, or is found out subsequently to have done so, it is not so much a bad example we are dealing with, but a reasonable ground for wondering whether the very existence of the coercive political order is, after all, a good thing, or at least whether there is any long-run reason for having patience with the existing coercive political order, attempting to make it better, and so on, rather than expecting the worst and trying something new. Official lawlessness greatly increases the case for revolution and overthrow, which is not a good thing.

Modern political coercive orders are understood in good part in terms of their structural legal features (the separation of powers, the electoral system if there is one, and so on). We do not have to follow Kelsen (2006) so far as to identify the state with law as a conceptual matter to see the central role law has in defining the substantive nature of our state. If the most fundamental structural law is not complied with, then while we may have a state, in the sense that we can point to those individuals and groups with a de facto near monopoly over the use of force, we will not have an institutional structure we can point to that might or might not deserve our allegiance over time; we will have only rulers. Noncompliance with ordinary law that applies to government has a similar effect, if extensive and flagrant enough. Any law that applies to a branch of government is an instance of the structure of the political order in operation. If the legislature legally can control the executive, within some areas, or there are constitutional limits on executive power, then those are defining features of the system. If we, the subjects of that system, cannot count on the executive to comply with law that applies to it, we cannot properly assess our reasons for supporting the overall political coercive order. The grounds for political obligation become opaque.

These remarks concern legal duties that apply to officials in their official capacity, rather than as private individuals. The instrumental case for compliance with law that applies to a person in his private capacity is perhaps also stronger for those who happen to be high officials than it is for the rest of us, but this difference is not the one to which I am attaching so much importance.[17] It should also be noted that in arguing for a strong instrumental moral case for officials in the executive branch to follow the law that applies to them in their official capacity, there is no suggestion that these officials ought to *enforce* the law in all particulars as against individuals. There are familiar and plausible reasons the executive should, in accordance with law, due process, and so on, exercise discretion in the enforcement of law.[18]

Consider next the legislature, and constitutional restrictions on valid legislation. If judicial review is not available, and the executive branch regards itself as bound to enforce law that is not struck down by the judicial branch, then the law will not be complied with unless majorities in the legislature constrain themselves. Once again, law here determines the basic institutional structure of the state. There is only one subject of this part of the law, and if it ignores the law or gives it little weight, then the institutional structure is changed.

Last, that the judicial branch should resolve disputes according to law, in all but the most extreme circumstances – such as would warrant an attempt to undermine a grossly unjust or illegitimate system from within – is not something that needs much argument. What else should it be doing?

---

[17] The greater instrumental case for compliance by officials considered in their private capacity is analogous to that for prominent nonofficial "leaders of society." See Raz (1979, 237–8) on the Archbishop of Canterbury.

[18] I am grateful here to Barbara Fried.

Prima facie duties can always be outweighed by unusual circumstances that provide a moral case for failing to comply. Perhaps during times of emergency the executive might justifiably flout settled law about the formal political process required in the conduct of war and about the means that may permissibly be used. The point is that the case in favor not only has to be strong on its own terms; it must also overcome the extremely powerful instrumental case in favor of governmental compliance with the law. We should not, I believe, become too exercised about these "exceptions." We should regard them for what they are, if they are: morally justified violations of law. Similarly, though there is considerable theoretical interest in figuring out the proper way to understand the legal regulation of emergency executive power, where the law itself suspends part of the law, in particular the prospects of maintaining the rule of law in such a context, none of this should affect the main conclusion that, barring unusual circumstances, members of the three branches of government have very strong instrumental reason to comply with law.

So even without considering the issue of character, we find a strong case for states to comply with law. The argument does, however, carry over to the motives and dispositions that officials would best have. The temptation to violate law, especially within the executive branch, is surely often very strong, and on occasion grounded in the best of aims. There is much to be said in favor and little to be said against a very strong standing disposition to comply – since true emergencies in their nature provide effective notice that the standing grounds for compliance may in this case be outweighed by other factors.

Now a typical reaction of the wise skeptic at this point would be to point out that, yes, it's all very well, but official lawlessness is widespread and the mere conclusion that governments ought to obey the law doesn't mean that they will. Of course that is so. And so it is of course extremely valuable to investigate the purely prudential reasons that may explain official submission to unenforced law. Even without complex modeling and speculation about the motives of officials, it is clear enough as a matter of common sense that officials frequently have strong self-interested reasons to comply with the law. They turn on reputation, the ability to secure their "policy aims," and so on (Levinson 2011). Moreover, wise constitutional designers from Madison on have been concerned to create institutional structures that will enhance the prudential reasons officials have for compliance. All of this might suggest that, although there is no institutional enforcement in the literal sense as against officials, in many or most legal systems, the incentives will be arranged such that officials will typically have very strong prudential reasons for compliance. As I discuss in the next chapter, it may be appropriate to regard this kind of deliberate adjusting of prices attached to choices as a kind of enforcement.

None of this undermines the central importance of determining whether, morally speaking, officials ought to comply.

Still, it is worth noting that much of the "positive" literature on compliance simply takes for granted that moral motivations will not be sufficient explanation for official compliance. The quest is, then, to produce more or less ingenious models that explain why nonetheless officials for the most part do comply. Properly understood, then, this literature asks a hypothetical question: Assuming that a desire or decision to do the right thing isn't the answer, why do officials comply? The truth is we simply do not know why officials comply with the law when they do; common sense, however, would suggest that a sense of moral duty plays a considerable role, much of the time.[19] That this motive should be shored up by clever constitutional design that attempts to align interest with compliance goes without saying.

I have emphasized the importance of government compliance with law, even in the absence of judicial determinations of the law's content. Given that the content of law is not always immediately clear, in such cases government may cloak noncompliance with disingenuous legal interpretation. This has been the subject of some debate in the United States in the wake of the "Torture Memos" during the administration of

---

[19] Though see Schauer (2010b, 2012) for a more skeptical view.

President George W. Bush. Various proposals have been made for non-court but independent bodies whose role it would be to determine the content of law as it applies to government (see, for example, Ackerman 2010). In the current U.S. context, such a proposal may make a great deal of sense, but this is not the place to pursue these issues. We should remember that even if actual courts were always available to declare the content of the law as it applied to the other two branches, the issue of compliance would remain alive.

The Focal Case

When it comes to the actions of states, individual cases of noncompliance with domestic law by higher-up officials can do great harm. The upshot here is that conventional thinking about what is the focal case of law, the municipal legal system effectively enforcing law as against individual subjects, is very misleading. It pushes to the margins law for states, both domestic and international. Since a central reason for being concerned about the content of law is that there are moral reasons to obey it, our focal case should to the contrary be that of the underenforced or unenforced law that applies to states. I continue with this line of thought in the next chapter, which addresses international law.

8 What Makes Law Law?

Law beyond the State

A System?

In the final few pages of *The Concept of Law*, Hart argued that international law might best be understood not as a legal system, the rules of which are valid in virtue of a rule of recognition, but rather as a set of rules that are valid or binding just in virtue of being accepted and functioning as such. Though international law could therefore be compared to "primitive" law, this did not mean that international law was any less law, or any less binding as law.[1] Hart's point, to the contrary, was that it was a mistake to assume that the hierarchical structure of domestic legal systems was essential to law, or a condition of its normative force.

Nonetheless, Hart's argument has not proved popular among international lawyers. As Martti Koskenniemi and Päivi Leino (2002, 558) put it:

> Hart's famous description of international law in terms of "rules that constitute not a system but a simple set" prompted generations of international lawyers to argue that a position which associated international law with "primitive law," denied its *grandeur* and was thus mistaken.

---

[1] Hart seems to have been widely misunderstood about this. See, for example, Koh's (1997, 2616) mysterious conclusion: "Hart defined the very notion of 'obedience' out of international law." For discussion of other cases of misunderstanding of Hart's theory by international legal theorists, see Lefkowitz (2008).

Half a century on, the profession has not forgotten Hart's discussion. In 2006, the International Law Commission (ILC) adopted the "Conclusions of the work of the Study Group on the Fragmentation of International Law: Difficulties Arising from the Diversification and Expansion of International Law" (ILC 2006a); Hart's claims are engaged in the Study Group's very first Conclusion:

> (1) *International law as a legal system.* International law is a legal system. Its rules and principles (i.e. its norms) act in relation to and should be interpreted against the background of other rules and principles. As a legal system, international law is not a random collection of such norms. There are meaningful relationships between them. Norms may thus exist at higher and lower hierarchical levels, their formulation may involve greater or lesser generality and specificity and their validity may date back to earlier or later moments in time.[2]

Hart evidently subscribed to the view that international law is all customary law. On this view, treaties are not a separate source of law, but are rather agreements legally binding in virtue of a principle of customary international law, *pacta sunt servanda.* Furthermore, Hart claims that there is no rule of recognition, and therefore no criterion of validity, that determines when a rule of customary international law is in force. It would have been possible for him to have made his point not by denying that international law has a rule of recognition, but by saying that it was all rule of recognition. As he writes, "The rules of the simple structure are, like the basic rule of the more advanced systems, binding if they are accepted and function as such" (235). Each rule of international law is in force, as it were, directly; there is no such thing as systemic validity, nothing *in virtue of which* each rule is in force. Just like the rule of recognition itself.[3]

---

[2] The other implicit target, of the last sentence, seems to be Weil 1983. The leader of the study group was Martti Koskenniemi, who "finalized" the long Report of the Study Group (ILC 2006b).

[3] This is why the so-called chronological puzzle of customary international law is matched by an exactly analogous puzzle for changes in the rule of recognition – as discussed in Chapter 3.

Hart seems to have been motivated by a desire to debunk what he saw as Kelsen's a priori assumption that all legal orders have the same structural features. Rather than assume that there must be a basic norm, Hart asks, why not look to see if there is one? (234; see also Lefkowitz 2008). Though Hart's reservations about Kelsen's essentialist inclinations are entirely reasonable, here they appear to lead him astray. For Kelsen, as we have seen, the *Grundnorm* has a function that Hart's rule of recognition does not – the function of animating a system of rules with genuine reason-giving force. For Kelsen, legal validity implies a genuine "ought," and the mere fact of acceptance that a practice is required by law obviously can't get you that. So Hart is wrong to imply that Kelsen's suggested *Grundnorm* for international law – "The States ought to behave as they have customarily behaved"(2006, 369) – is redundant and silly. It is not redundant for Kelsen, just because in his legal theory some such "presupposed" ought is required to get from facts to valid (in his sense) norms.

It is hard to disagree that if we use "validity" in Hart's sense that implies no objective reason-giving force, then a rule's being part of a simple set is irrelevant to its potential legal validity or its reason-giving force. And that was one main point Hart wished to make. But Hart also made the substantive legal claim that there are no "general criteria of validity for international law" (236), and for this he provided little if any argument.

Article 38 of the Statute of the International Court of Justice sets out three primary sources of international law: treaties, custom, and "general principles of law recognized by civilized countries." This Article is still generally regarded as a canonical statement of the sources of international law, even if it is perhaps no longer exhaustive, and even if the third source has played little role in the jurisprudence of the court.[4] In any event, regardless of the Statute, if anything is accepted among

---

[4] See Thirlway. That principles of law found in the domestic law of "civilized countries" are part of international law is clearly a substantive criterion of validity.

international lawyers, it is that the sources of international law include custom and treaties. The question is whether Hart is right that treaties are not a separate source of law, but just contracts binding in virtue of a customary legal rule, and right also that customary legal rules are valid just because they are directly accepted as such, not because of the satisfaction of some separate accepted criterion of validity.

Taking the second question first, the Statute puts forward the orthodox view that customary law requires a state practice coupled with an *opinio juris*: "international custom, as evidence of a general practice accepted as law." Since in Hart's view a rule of recognition exists in virtue of being practiced and accepted, we can understand why he could see no daylight between the criterion and the particular rules that it validates. But in fact the criterion is doing some work. A criterion for the existence of customary law would do no work in the Hartian scheme if its content were "those rules which are accepted and function as legal rules among legal officials."[5] Once a rule is accepted and functioning as a legal rule among the relevant people, just because it is and not for any reason of pedigree, it is already in force – that's the end of the line in the Hartian account of validity.

But now, in the first place, what matters for customary international law is the practice and opinions of states, not the beliefs and attitudes of international legal officials generally (Lefkowitz 2008). Second, there is a substantive inquiry to be had, as the criterion is currently understood, about the interplay between state practice and *opinio juris*. There are questions about what exactly would demonstrate an *opinio juris*, whether it could predate a practice, how uniform the practice must be, whether and how the two requirements could be balanced against each other (less practice, more *opinio* and vice versa), and so on (Besson 2010, Tasioulas

---

[5] Using the broader account I discuss in Chapter 3, we should replace "legal officials" with "those with a life in international law, such as judges on international tribunals, judges on domestic courts, officials in international organizations, domestic executive-branch legal officials, and professors of international law."

2007, Thirlway 2006). State practice plus *opinio juris* is simply not the same as "accepted and functions as a binding rule" among legal officials.

On the question of whether treaties are a separate source of law, *pacta sunt servanda* can certainly be regarded, and traditionally has often been regarded, as a rule of customary international law. This is defensible as a matter of logic, but it also seems somewhat misleading as it assimilates all treaties to the model of ordinary contract. Though Hart himself is inclined to think that ordinary contracts between individuals involve the exercise of "limited legislative powers by individuals"(96), that is a rather peculiar view. Ordinary contracts are agreements that are legally enforceable; that entering into a contract affects my legal obligations does not mean that I have made law. Multilateral treaties, on the other hand, such as the UN Charter, the UN Convention on the Law of the Sea, the agreements that establish the World Trade Organization and the entire legal order of international trade – these agreement are naturally regarded as law creating. A particularly clear example is the UN Convention on Contracts for the International Sale of Goods (CISG), which operates as commercial code for international commercial sales. It is hard to keep a clear grip on the idea that, in applying the terms of the CISG, a domestic court is enforcing its national government's international contractual obligations. For many treaties, then, it is more natural to treat them as sources of law in their own right, rather than enforceable agreements under a customary rule (Payandeh 2011, 982–5). Still, it must be said that that is all it is – a more natural way of talking. There does not seem to be anything more at stake in the issue of whether the legal force of treaties derives from a norm of customary law validated by the criterion of validity for customary international law or rather directly from a distinct criterion of validity.

Either way, it seems that a Hartian should allow that there is at least one criterion of validity for rules of international law, and that there is therefore a substantive rule of recognition for international law.

But suppose Hart were right that there are no criteria of validity for international law and therefore that validity in international law is direct rather than systemic. In that case, as Hart says, a rule of recognition would be just an "empty restatement of the fact that a set of rules are in fact observed by states" (236). Since this restatement of all the rules of customary international law would tell us the content of the international legal order, in what sense would it be empty? It would be empty because the rule of recognition would not set out criteria in virtue of which the norms of international law were norms of international law. The rule of recognition would therefore not ground a system of law in the sense that Hart had in mind – a normative order in which the validity of lower-level norms was systematically derived from higher-level norms.

So we can say that, had Hart been right that there were no criteria of validity in international law, international law would not be a system, in his specific sense. But this is entirely compatible with international law being a system in the sense that is proclaimed by the first conclusion of the ILC Study Group (Payandeh 2011, 992). A set of rules that have direct rather than derived validity can nonetheless be connected in that they refer to each other and develop in the context of the existence of the others. Within international law there are centuries-old customary rules for dealing with conflicts among rules, such as *lex specialis derogate lex generali*. These connections among the rules (discussed further later in this chapter) enable us to say, in a sense entirely different and much more important than Hart's, that this group of legal rules makes up a legal system. In Raz's classification, we could say that so understood, international law is a system of "interlocking norms" (Raz 1999, 111) even if, because there are no criteria of legal validity, it is not a system in Hart's sense.

As I said at the outset, it is clear enough why Hart's conclusion that there is no international legal system in his sense does not lead him to think that international law is any less real, or potentially binding. We now see that this conclusion also provides no grounds for attributing to him the view (to use the words of the Study Group again) that "international law is ... a random collection of ... norms" with no "meaningful relationships between them." Nonetheless, Hart certainly did not try to forestall such an interpretation. And in any case, international lawyers are quite right that he did think that international law was defective in some way.

In saying that international law is a "primitive" legal order, Hart associates it with three disadvantages of primitive law described earlier in his book: those of uncertainty, static rules, and the lack of an authoritative body that can resolve all disputes (92–3). As international law lacks a legislature and a court of compulsory and general jurisdiction, it is not difficult to conclude that it has the second and third defects (if that is what they are). Hart's main concern was evidently the lack of an international legislature. When explaining what it means for a legal order to lack criteria of validity, he writes:

> In the simpler form of society we must wait and see whether a rule gets accepted as a rule or not; in a system with a basic rule of recognition we can say before a rule is actually made, that it *will* be valid *if* it conforms to the requirements of the rule of recognition. (235)

This statement evidently reflects Hart's view that treaties are not a distinct source of law, but rather contracts binding in virtue of a norm of customary international law. But he goes on to suggest that if one day multilateral treaties bind nonparties, "such treaties would in fact be legislative enactments and international law would have distinct criteria of validity for its rules" (236). What's odd here is that in Hart's legal theory, the primary thing a legislative process gives us is a rule of change. The rule of recognition, by contrast, is supposed to deal with uncertainty, and the existence of a rule of recognition is compatible with the lack of a rule of change.[6]

Perhaps the main reason these last pages of *The Concept of Law* are confusing is that there is a disconnect between Hart's theoretical focus on

---

[6] Waldron (2009b) puts pressure on the need for rules of recognition in the Hartian system, suggesting that all the work can be done by rules of change. His argument is compelling for much of domestic law, but there is a residual need for a rule of recognition in the case of an entirely static legal order that does not recognize any canonical process for changing its content.

the rule of recognition and what appears to be his main substantive complaint – that international law, lacking a legislature and (as he appears to have believed) rules of change generally, is a static legal order. It's as if he was trying to kill two birds with one stone – rejecting Kelsen's insistence on a basic norm for international law while at the same time bringing out international law's "primitive" lack of rules of change – but he missed.

But now, does international law make up a legal system or not? It depends on which sense of "system" is worth worrying about. One might of course decide to reserve the label "system" for institutionally more complex legal orders, perhaps those with legislatures, or those with the right kind of courts, but it would still be misleading to characterize what is not a system in that sense as a mere random collection of unconnected rules. To use Raz's (1999, 123) terminology again, we might better characterize domestic law as an "institutionalized" system as opposed to international law's system of interlocking norms. Or we might simply say that these two legal systems differ in their institutional structures in obvious ways.

But there is more at stake here than a choice between classificatory schemes. That there is a sense of "system" that matters in connection with international law is brought home by the discussion in recent decades of the issue of fragmentation, which was the topic of the ILC Study Group.

"Legislative" multilateral treaties have proliferated in the past half century, and some of them create organizational structures that can be seen as continuing to make law beyond the treaty-making stage (Alvarez . 2005). Furthermore, multilateral treaties can be picked up by customary international law and for that reason bind nonparties in the course of time. Nonparties still cannot be automatically bound, just because the treaty is in effect, so we do not have the "legislative enactments" Hart refers to; but an enormous amount of new law has been made since Hart wrote nonetheless. Though some of it can count at least partly as codification of customary international law, much of it cannot. Salient multilateral treaties since Hart wrote include the Vienna Convention on the Law of Treaties, the UN Convention on the Law of the Sea, the Marrakech agreements that established the World Trade Organization (WTO), the CISG, and the Rome Statute of the International Criminal Court (ICC). Most significant of all, perhaps, is the emergence of an entire new supranational legal system in Europe.

Ironically, given Hart's discussion, the very fruitfulness of the mechanism of lawmaking by treaty led many commentators to see a danger of fragmentation in international law – lots of legal change leading to less rather than more system. This anxiety was expressed by successive presidents of the ICJ in 1999 and 2000, who focused especially on the fact that many of these new treaty-based international organizations have their own tribunals for the resolution of disputes (Koskenniemi and Leino 2002). Important new adjudicatory bodies include the International Tribunal for the Law of the Sea, the Dispute Settlement Body of the WTO, the International Criminal Tribunals for the former Yugoslavia and Rwanda, the International Criminal Court (ICC), and of course the European Court of Justice and the European Court of Human Rights.

The worry about fragmentation is that these new sources of law, with their own adjudicatory bodies, might break off from international law generally. International law could split apart so that, say, trade law – though it is law, and it is international – is not plausibly thought to be a part of a wider international legal system. This worry can be pitched at the normative and the institutional levels. At the normative level, the question is whether there remains a coherent overall normative structure to international law that can accommodate the "diversification and expansion" of international law and provide legal grounds to resolve conflicts. We could say that this is the question of whether international law can remain a single normative system that, in principle, could be in force. The institutional question relates to the proliferation of new subject-specific adjudicatory bodies. The apparent institutional danger is that even if in principle there is a single system of international law capable of correct interpretation, judicial practice will diverge so greatly among the new bodies, leading to forum shopping and divergence in the conduct of states, that we will no

longer be able to claim that that single system of international law is in
fact in force; rather, several distinct legal systems will be in force.

Would this matter? It may be wondered why fragmentation is a cause
for concern at all (Kingsbury 1999). One might believe that only a single unitary international legal system is conceptually possible – perhaps
because all legal systems are thought necessarily to claim both supremacy and universality in their subject matter jurisdiction and so only one
system can be in effect at the same time. But it is not hard to understand
the idea of distinct legal orders relating to distinct subject areas, and not
relating to each other, all being generally complied with by states. If, say,
trade law and environmental law made up such distinct systems, and their
norms did yield conflicting accounts of states' obligations, there would
be no all-things-considered answer to the question of what "the law"
required states to do. This would leave a practical normative problem for
states; there might be a right thing to do, all things considered, but that is
compatible with there being no single legal answer. This kind of conflict is
in fact quite familiar – indigenous law may provide a different answer to
state law, which may be different from regional law, which may be different from international law. And of course at the horizontal level we are
familiar with conflicts of laws between different domestic jurisdictions
and among different courts in the same jurisdiction – bankruptcy courts
and courts of general jurisdiction, for example. In most such familiar
cases, legal doctrine resolves the conflict, and so the distinguishable legal
orders do in fact relate to each other via that doctrine. But take away the
doctrine that legally regulates the conflict, and the legal orders would not
disappear in a puff of smoke.

Now international law as it currently is seems neither to consist in
distinct international legal systems or regimes that do not relate to each
other via rules and methods of interpretation that resolve conflicts, nor a
single international legal system where there is always a single answer to
the question of what "international law" says about the matter. It is some-
where in the middle. International law does not present itself as, in principle, free of conflict between, say, different treaty regimes; but neither

are techniques lacking to reduce or avoid conflict in many or most cases (Crawford and Nevill 2012). At the very least, all treaties are connected by the principles of interpretation found in the Vienna Convention on the Law of Treaties, which is part of customary international law. The question is whether it would be better to be moving to a genuinely unified single legal order or in the other direction; or whether it doesn't matter either way.

On the face of it, it seems likely that fragmentation of international law into distinct legal systems would be a bad development, because it would reduce the instrumental value of international legal practice overall. As discussed later in this chapter, the basis of states' obligations to obey international law lies in the good that a practice of general obedience with law may do. This value seems likely to be increased if there is a single legal order covering all subject areas, primarily because self-interested or moral allegiance to the system as a whole can promote compliance with those areas of legal regulation that impose net costs on individual states. If a violation of environmental law is considered a violation of the very same law, in a broad sense, as trade law, that's all for the good as far as the environment is concerned.

Now of course this assumes that international legal governance is a good thing – in the sense that we would do better working with it, trying to make it better, than pulling it down. But even apart from that, the situation is more complicated than it may at first seem (Koskenniemi 2012). For example, champions of international human rights law may not welcome attempts by WTO tribunals to find an all-things-considered legal answer where trade law and human rights law speak on the same subject because this may lead human rights law in an unwelcome direction (Alston 2002). By the same token, however, making law via multilateral treaties with very narrowly defined subject matter is a mechanism suited, and, it could be argued, designed, to increase the power of the most powerful states, especially, of course, the United States. Among other factors, this way of proceeding prevents weaker states from forming effective cross-issue coalitions (Benvenisti and Downs 2007).

Some of these points turn on both the institutional and the normative aspects of fragmentation. The ILC Study Group declined to address the institutional side of the issue. One can understand why, as everything turns on the practice of the various tribunals; a full survey would obviously be an enormously complex undertaking. But it is clear that there is no reason of principle why a proliferation of adjudicatory bodies must lead to diverging interpretations of the law. After all, the International Court of Justice (ICJ) never has had compulsory jurisdiction, so it is not as if an existing hierarchical system on the domestic model has been replaced with a horizontal free for all. The question is whether the new landscape of multiple tribunals of specialized jurisdiction has in fact increased disagreement and uncertainty about the content of law. Here there is debate. Many international lawyers and legal theorists are rather optimistic on this front (see, e.g., Pauwelyn 2003). Much is made of "dialogue" among national, supranational, and international courts and the desire of judges or those assuming an adjudicatory role to try to agree with one another (see Burke-White 2005). For others, the distinct institutional settings and affiliations of adjudicators on different tribunals inevitably push in the other direction, toward fragmentation (Alvarez 2008).

On the normative question, the forty-two Conclusions and the accompanying five-hundred-odd-page Report of the Study Group present an elegant and compelling legal argument to the effect that international law, especially as expressed in the Vienna Convention on the Law of Treaties, contains principles of interpretation and conflicts rules sufficient to justify the statement in the first Conclusion that "as a legal system, international law is not a random collection of ... norms." In other words, for many and perhaps most cases of conflicting legal sources, international law does provide a single answer.

This conclusion is also not uncontroversial. But this is not the right place to look further into the issue, for the main point to make is that whether international law is a single unified normative system is a doctrinal question to be resolved by looking at the norms of international law that are common to various different subparts of it. Different legal theories, different theories of the grounds of law, will approach this inquiry differently, of course, and it seems plausible to think that non-positivists would more easily find a single system than positivists. But that also depends on whether it would, morally speaking, be better if there were a single system; and this too, as we have seen, is a complex question that cannot be fully addressed here.

Supposing international law is a single system, there remain complex and deeply important issues of how that system interacts with other systems. There is rather obviously not just one legal system in the world, with all conflicts resolvable according to rules of hierarchy and interpretation provided by that single legal order. The current legal landscape for member states of the European Union is most naturally described as involving three distinct legal systems (Dickson 2008; though see Kumm 2012). This raises questions of hierarchy and conflict resolution that particular states and particular courts will have to resolve without a single source of purely legal guidance. Was the ECJ right to hold in the 2008 *Kadi* case that European regulations implementing a UN Security Council resolution concerning the freezing of assets of those on a "terror list" were invalid for being inconsistent with fundamental rights found in European law (see de Búrca 2010)? What about the similar stance taken by the German Constitutional Court with respect to European law in relation to the German Constitution? (see Kumm 2005). The issues here are doctrinal and jurisdictional, but also, for both courts and executive branches, political. These kinds of issues seem likely to grow ever more important as and if legal systems beyond the state continue to proliferate (see Besson 2010; Twining 2009).

Law? and More Law?: The Question of Enforcement

It may be a system of norms, more or less institutionalized, but is it law? The old question of whether international law is really law relates to the classification of distinct types of normative orders. What makes a legal

order distinct from, say, "positive morality," as Austin (1995, 112) charac-
terized international law?

This is a question about the nature of law or the content of the concept of law, but it is distinct from the issue of the grounds of law. There are
some connections, of course. Positivists about the grounds of law will be
disinclined to accept as a criterion for the existence of a legal system that
the norms of the system are sufficiently just, or otherwise good. If you are
convinced that a rule's validity is one thing, its merit or demerit and reason-giving force quite another, you are likely to feel the same way about
the system as a whole. Similarly, if you hold that legal rights and duties
are real moral rights and duties, gross systemic injustice would appear to
disqualify some political coercive orders from being legal systems right
from the start. So it is no surprise that positivists and Dworkinian nonpositivists have argued about whether there was a legal system in Nazi
Germany, even though their primary debate is about the grounds of law
(see, e.g., Dworkin, 1986, 101–8).

But other suggested criteria for the existence of law have nothing to
do with the relation between law and morality. Even Lon Fuller's account
of law as a distinctive kind of system of governance is entirely compatible
with a positivist outlook, so long as we treat the "inner morality of law"
as an implication of his account, rather than its motivation (see Rundle
2012; Shapiro 2011, 392–5). It is intuitively appealing to think that law as
a mode of governance is distinctive for treating its subjects as responsible
deliberative agents (Waldron 2008). A mode of governance that violates
Fuller's principles of prospectivity, publicity, constancy, generality, and so
on is not one that offers people norms that they may choose to accept,
and it is easy to feel that it is therefore inappropriate to call it a "legal
system" – even without engaging the issue of whether it is morally better
to govern people as agents.

The criteria for the existence of a legal system that have been raised
against international law typically relate to its supposed institutional
deficiencies and are therefore similarly neutral as between positivists and
nonpositivists. We can leave aside Austin's demotion of international law

to positive morality on account of there being no sovereign to do the commanding. And few are inclined to argue anymore that the lack of a legislature or a hierarchical court system with compulsory jurisdiction is disqualifying.[7] But there is one apparent difference between global and domestic law that does continue to get attention. The problem for the status of law beyond the state, for many, is not that it lacks a sovereign to do the commanding, but that it lacks a sovereign – an executive branch – to do the enforcing.

It is important to distinguish the issue of enforcement from that of compliance. From the point of view of legal theory, it is clear enough that a legal system is not *in force* if it is not generally complied with. This is just Kelsen's criterion of effectiveness, which is one of the few aspects of his theory that should be acceptable to everyone. This is an entirely separate issue from the place of enforcement or coercion in an account of the nature of law. But the two have been run together somewhat in international legal theory.

Is international law generally complied with? Louis Henkin's (1979, 47) commonsense observation that "almost all nations observe almost all principles of international law and almost all of their obligations most of the time" has been confronted with two distinct responses.

There is, first, the attempt to test this statement by empirical studies of particular areas of international law. Though there is much to think about methodologically here, the results so far do not dramatically undermine Henkin's commonsense guess (see Beth Simmons 2010 for an excellent review). If Henkin's guess is right, it supports – what again seems to be common sense – that international law is effective in Kelsen's sense. It is a system in force.

A very different line of response insists that compliance in the sense of acting in conformity with legal rules is not at all interesting. We need to know whether international law *makes a difference*, it is said, in the

---

[7] For a compelling debate between legal anthropologists about the idea that law requires a state, see Roberts (2005) and Pirie (2010).

sense of affecting states and other global legal subjects' incentives. Here rational choice and game theory enter international legal theory. Jack Goldsmith and Eric Posner's (2005) analysis leads them to conclude:

> The best explanation for when and why states comply with international law is not that states have internalized international law, or have a habit of complying with it, or are drawn by its moral pull, but simply that states act out of self-interest. (225)

Goldsmith and Posner's theoretical argument seems on the face of it question begging since self-interest is defined as preference maximization and states are assumed to have no "preference" for compliance with international law (Golove 2005–6). But the argument is important for being part of a more general turn in international legal theory, one that tests the worth of international law in terms of the difference it makes to states' calculations of self-interest, narrowly construed (see Howse and Teitel 2010).

The traditional idea in legal philosophy that a legal order must be generally complied with if it is to be in force leaves entirely open why exactly legal subjects might comply; what matters is compliance, not its ground.[8] For these purposes, empirical studies of the behavior of states are of course directly relevant; modeling that aims to show that only self-interest ever motivates compliance is beside the point. So what is the purpose of such analyses? In the case of Goldsmith and Posner, the overall aim seems to be to undermine the "conventional wisdom" that states act on the belief that international law has moral force and that this belief is true (185).

More interesting for legal philosophy is the methodologically similar approach of a friend of international law, Andrew Guzman. Guzman

---

[8] Tamanaha (2001, 145–6) appears to understand compliance to mean that legal subjects "obey" law in the sense that they act in accordance with it because they believe they have some kind of standing reason to do what is legally required. He is right to reject efficacy understood in that way; it would not be a remotely plausible criterion for the existence of a legal system. We might, for example, hope that most of us act in accordance with most of criminal law for reasons that have nothing to do with law. (For relevant remarks, see Raz 1994, 343.) The criminal legal system is nonetheless in effect.

(2008) argues that international law generally does provide narrowly self-interested reasons for compliance, because of the role of what he calls the three Rs of compliance – reputation, reciprocity, and retaliation. But he notes that so-called soft law – non-legally binding agreements and declarations such as the Basle banking accords, the Helsinki accords, declarations of the UN General Assembly, and so on – may provide exactly the same reasons for compliance (even before they become the basis of new customary law, if they do). He goes on to claim that this result requires a revision in our understanding of the nature of international law. International law, for Guzman, includes any supranational agreement or perceived obligation that changes the incentives states confront (Guzman 2002, 1882).

What has happened here is that, even though skeptically minded international legal theorists are no longer comfortable simply asserting that international law is not really law because it lacks a central institutionalized enforcement apparatus on the model of the domestic state, many apparently feel that something else must be performing the same function for there to be law in any recognizable sense. For Guzman, the claim is that a distinctive characteristic of a legal system is that its demands come accompanied by prices for noncompliance. Guzman labels his approach a "compliance" theory of international law, but it is really all about enforcement.

Guzman's approach is over-inclusive to the extent of being eliminativist, as it simply labels as "legal" any norm with which self-interest counsels compliance. "A vocabulary is needed to distinguish those obligations of states that affect incentives and behavior, and the term law seems to be sufficient for that purpose"(2002, 1878). On such a view, a theory of legal sources is a theory that enables states to know when others expect them to do something and that there will be a price to pay for not doing it (see Guzman 2008, 195).

It will obviously not do to identify law with all norms that are enforced in the sense that a price is attached to noncompliance. (I make a promise that is not enforceable under contract law. Am I nonetheless legally required to perform if nonperformance will ruin my reputation?) But Guzman's approach is helpful in bringing out a broader idea of enforcement, one that goes beyond the coercive power of centralized institutions to include any situation where noncompliance attracts penalties. Along these lines, Oona Hathaway and Scott Shapiro (2011) propose to show that international law does satisfy the demand that legal systems enforce their norms. It's just that in the case of international law, enforcement is not carried out by legal institutions themselves but rather, for the most part, by states, and it often takes the form of the withdrawal of benefits of membership in some institutional scheme – what they call "outcasting" – and usually not brute force.

Hathaway and Shapiro for the most part describe the external sanctioning measures provided for by specialized treaty regimes, such as the WTO. But the overall structure they describe has a long history in the international law of state responsibility. This body of doctrine explains the responsibility of states in terms of breaches of obligations of international law, prescribes obligations of repair, and allows in some circumstances the enforcement mechanism of countermeasures, which are defined as the nonperformance of obligations that the harmed state otherwise has to the noncomplying state (see Crawford and Olleson 2010).

What is important to Hathaway and Shapiro is that the international legal order itself provides for – permits or requires – the sanctioning actions in question. The enforcement of international law in this way goes beyond the (as it were) natural effects on reputation, and so on, that are equally present in the case of non-legally binding agreements. Is this what lies behind the intuitive connection that so many feel between law and coercion – a sense that a legal order must itself in some way provide for sanctions that will encourage compliance, even if no centralized enforcement institutions are in place?

If this proposal means that any particular legal norm must be backed by sanctions contemplated by the legal order itself, we must reject it. As noted in the previous chapter, there are no sanctions specified for breaches of domestic constitutional law by the executive branch. And as

Hathaway and Shapiro themselves note, there is no outcasting sanction available for standalone human rights or environmental treaties. Their response to this fact is to treat it as just a matter of institutional design – a human rights regime could be bundled in with other, mutually beneficial schemes, as is the case with the European Convention on Human Rights (321). But of course the lack of an international police force could also be cast as just a matter of institutional design. Moreover, this suggests that, *in the meantime*, the legal status of the standalone and not materially mutually beneficial treaty regimes is in doubt. This doesn't seem at all plausible.

On the other hand, it also does not seem plausible to sever the link between law and coercion entirely. So perhaps we should say this. It is not that status as law requires provision for effective enforcement. It is that when it comes to law we would regard it as obviously appropriate for provision to be made within the normative order itself for effective enforcement. Properly regulated third-party enforcement is always in principle appropriate. This is precisely what we do not think for the case of an agreement that the parties expressly announce is not legally binding. If there is to be any insistence on a close connection between law and enforcement, I believe that it must take this form. One thing that is distinctive about legal systems is that effective coercive enforcement is considered appropriate in the nature of things. Thus I agree with Grant Lamond (2001, 55) that the link between a legal system and coercion is, as he puts it, justificatory rather than constitutive: "Law claims the right to reinforce its directives with coercive measures." Of course substantive conditions of legitimacy have to be satisfied if enforcement is justified, but the thought that law presents itself as a set of legitimate demands that, things being in order, may justifiably be enforced in accordance with rules and standards provided for by law itself, with brute force where appropriate, rings true. None of this means that, in situations where legitimate enforcement is not possible or practicable, the status of a norm as legal is diminished. But it does help to distinguish law from other normative systems.

There is a connection here with Locke's position that there is a natural right, in the state of nature, to punish violations of the law of nature. I agree with Anscombe (1990) that this confuses the issue of whether I deserve punishment with the issue of who may inflict it. "One may be wronged in a secondary way by getting one's deserts at the hands of someone who had no right so to inflict them" (163). What a third party may do to me if I act (morally) wrongly is a substantive moral question; but it seems clear that the mere fact that I have acted wrongly doesn't automatically justify enforcement measures by just anyone. By contrast, if it is (legitimate) law I have violated and the law itself specifies the proper agency and nature of punishment, the appropriateness of some coercive response is taken for granted – though there will always be questions about the justice of the type and measure of the sanction.

In the moral realm, we need to ask: Do we have the right to get involved and start trying to change people's behavior by imposing sanctions of some kind? (Sometimes we do, sometimes we don't.) In the legal realm, we don't ask whether the appropriate people have the right to impose sanctions for noncompliance with law, but rather whether the conduct in question was properly subject to legal regulation in the first place.[9]

To pursue the question of what distinguishes the legal from other normative orders from a different direction, and perhaps to justify raising it in the first place, we can consider the case of emerging law. The most important and interesting discussion in contemporary international legal theory concerns what is usually referred to as "global governance."

---

[9] This is where the very fruitful discussion between Anthony Duff and his critics about the proper scope of the "criminal law's business" fits in. That discussion takes for granted that legitimate criminal law can impose sanctions. If we conclude that it would be wrong for the authorities to get involved, we conclude that the conduct is wrongly criminalized. See Duff (2007) and the essays in Cruft, Kramer, and Reiff (2011). My remarks do not engage that substantive dispute.

The precise scope of this term is itself the subject of scholarly articles, but the rough idea is to highlight the impact made by international organizations on the policy options of states and the lives of people globally (Kingsbury 2009; Kingsbury, Krisch, & Stewart 2005; von Bogdandy, Dann, & Goldmann 2008; Walker & de Búrca 2007). It is important that while these institutions may be the creatures of treaties and so too of international law in the classical sense, that is just one possibility. They may also be informal club-like arrangements between states' executive branches, hybrid public/private institutions, or even fully private institutions. The political issue raised by this aspect of globalization is that there is a global institutional sphere of great impact that is not necessarily subject to the control of states and so potentially lacks even so much accountability as customary and treaty law may have. As we have already noted, even organizations that are created by treaty, such as the UN Security Council, have taken on rule-creating and decisional functions that are not under the continuing "legislative" control of the parties to the Charter (Alvarez 2005).

There are at least two questions concerning the relationship between law and this change in the way the world is governed. The first is the extent to which it makes sense to think of the rules and decisions made by these various bodies as legal rules and decisions. The other is whether and how law might assert some control over all this consequential institutional activity.

The answer to the first question will depend on the organization in question. Thus when the Security Council places a person on its "terror list," directing member states to freeze that person's assets, this is regarded as a decision with legal force. If it were not, the ECJ's *Kadi* decision would not have become a celebrated case. At the other extreme, decisions by the purely private International Standardization Organization (ISO), though they can have pervasive impact both on domestic law and decisions by treaty-based international organizations, surely do not have legal force. If they did, so too would decisions of private ratings agencies, such as Moody's. Or consider the decisions, especially the anticipated decisions, of (global) bond traders, that impose (at least perceived) rigid constraints on the range of feasible economic and social policies for most states.

That it is an NGO rather than a corporation or a collective of independent individuals obviously does not in itself make the ISO's standards law, nor does the fact that it is made up of representatives from all countries in the world. Nothing could make the ISO standards law since they available for a fee, on a take it or leave it basis. The issue of what to make of noncompliance simply doesn't arise since there could be no such thing. It is true that ISO standards are incorporated into legal regulation, for example through the WTO (Kingsbury, Krisch, & Stewart 2005, 23), but that fact does not make the standards themselves legally binding – no more so than regulation of banks and other financial institutions that refers to and incorporates the decisions of private ratings agencies makes Moody's a lawmaker.

Of course, that an organization's decisions do not have legal force does not mean that it would be inappropriate to regulate them by law. Especially since the financial crisis of 2008, private ratings agencies are regulated by U.S. law. Once our attention is broadened from lawmaking entities to any global organization or activity that may have an impact on people's lives, however, it is natural to wonder why the focus of the global governance discussion is on international organizations of various kinds, rather than on any activity, private or public, individual or collective, that affects people's lives globally. But leaving that aside, the current question is this: If legal regulation of an international organization is thought appropriate, how should it be done?

In the case of decisions by bodies that are creatures of treaty regimes, one obvious solution would be legislative change – revise the treaty to mandate whatever procedural rules on decision making we believe to be appropriate. But apart from being unlikely in practice, that would not cover precisely the cases that are of most concern from the point of view of accountability, those international organizations that are not creatures of law. To a certain extent, the impact of such organizations could be regulated at the point of incorporation into legal regulation – at the point at which ISO standards are appealed to in trade law, for example. But the impact of these kinds of organizations is not exhausted by their incorporation into law. We need a broader, or more inclusive approach.

There are a number of inclusive approaches currently under discussion. There is the idea that the organizations in question make up a "global administrative space" that is appropriately regulated by "global administrative law" on the model of domestic administrative law (Kingsbury, Krisch, & Stewart 2005). Another option is to broaden the understanding of what has traditionally been called international institutional law (von Bogdandy, Dunn, & Goldmann 2008).

This whole field is extremely complex, and I cannot hope to do it justice. So I will just use as an example the global administrative law model. Here the claim is that accountability for the effects of the actions of these multifarious international organizations requires compliance with such norms as transparency, consultation, participation, rationality, and review (Kingsbury 2009). In the absence of more robust democratic accountability, compliance with these norms of process would obviously be a good thing. But the proposal is that a global administrative *law* is emerging, and my question is what exactly that means in a context where conventional jurisprudence currently recognizes no such law.

There ought to be a law. In a context of effective enforcement, this most naturally means that "the authorities" should put a stop to it. What does it mean in the absence of enforcement?

That there ought to be a (global administrative) law, or that one is emerging, must mean more than that these global institutions, since they have such a significant impact, and since they are not subject to democratic control, really ought to comply with certain formal and procedural standards in decision making. After all, if that's true, it's already true. Perhaps there is a range of equally acceptable procedures and it matters that all the relevant organizations adhere to the same ones; but a proposal that all the relevant entities get together and solve this coordination problem would still not bring us to a role for law. That there ought to be a law must mean more than that it would be good if the relevant decision makers practiced some code of "IO ethics"; to say that new law is emerging is evidently to say more than that people are starting to converge in their ethical views.

The question, as Jutta Brunnée and Stephen Toope (2010, 20) put it, is "What value does 'law' add?" Their own answer is that if a normative practice satisfies the requirements of legality, or the rule of law, as set out in Fuller's account, this alone is sufficient to qualify the norms as legal norms, and the value that adds is that the system of governance is more deserving of "fidelity" (27). This answer cannot be right, however, because all sorts of normatively structured cooperative practices could satisfy Fuller's formal requirements. Those requirements may be necessary for law, but they obviously are not sufficient.

It is also obvious that the various institutional criteria (courts, legislatures, enforcement agencies) now generally rejected for the case of public international law are not helpful in this case. Comprehensiveness and a claim to supremacy, two criteria for the existence of a legal system suggested by Raz (1999, 150–2), seem question begging in the case of law beyond the state – even, given the prospect of fragmentation, for public international law. What is left?

Brian Tamanaha's (2001, 133–70) discussion of criteria that have been suggested to mark the boundary between law and other kinds of normative order in effect concludes that nothing is left. Tamanaha does want to acknowledge such a boundary, he does not want any old thing to count as law; but the only criterion he can accept is a purely nominal one: "*Law is whatever people identify and treat through their social practices as 'law' (or droit, recht, etc.)*" (166).

Though Tamanaha's skeptical remarks about proposed substantive criteria for distinguishing legal from other forms of normative order seem compelling one by one, the position he arrives at is not plausible. For one thing, it makes translation puzzling – perhaps we are comfortable about "droit" and "Recht," but how would we choose between "law" and "mores" when translating some language for the first time? If no beliefs at all are associated with the word "law," we have nothing to go by.[10] More important, it leaves us with nothing to think about when we ask ourselves whether an activity or practice ought to be legally regulated. Suppose we suggest that there should be a new supranational legal system, addressing issues both of human rights and trade in our region. What exactly are we saying? Something different from the claim that states really ought to play fair when it comes to trade and to respect the rights of their subjects, no doubt, but what?

Might the right response be that while none of the criteria just mentioned is necessary or sufficient on its own, the group of them together do determine, in a loose and aggregative way, the boundary between law and other kinds of normative order? If there is a lot on all these dimensions you have law; not much and you don't. This is the idea of fixing reference with a "cluster" of descriptions, which is a version of the criterial approach to concepts mentioned in Chapter 6. The trouble is, it seems that even total failure to satisfy *any* of these criteria (no legislature, courts, centralized enforcement, or claims to comprehensiveness and supremacy) doesn't rule out the idea of global administrative law. Similarly, if public international law did fragment, and international environmental law, say, were properly regarded as a separate regime, it would not satisfy any of the criteria.

There are more criteria that could be discussed, but I will not here attempt a comprehensive treatment (for relevant discussion, see Yankah 2008). Rather, my hope is that this review of the issue of what makes law law in the context of calls for new law will provide intuitive support for the position arrived at earlier. When we say that there ought to be a law, we are not necessarily saying that existing authorities should put a stop to some conduct. But part of what we are saying does seem to be that we want the kind of normative order that would appropriately (where feasible) include some rules designed to encourage compliance, and that it would be right and proper for the authorities (if there are any) to enforce the norms coercively in the ordinary course of events. We have in mind a

---

[10] See Twining (2003, 223–31) for an effective sustained critique of Tamanaha's proposal.

normative order whose rules are generally taken to be and are presented as being appropriately enforced – if feasible and done in accordance with rules of that very order. That's one main difference law makes, one value that it adds. And that is why, I venture, you would want a global administrative law if you are concerned about the impact of unaccountable global institutions on our lives, rather than just IO ethics.[11]

In effect, to call for new legal norms is to express confidence that any moral objection to enforcing them could be met. Whether enforcement should or will in fact take place will turn on issues of feasibility and institutional design.

Of course, to say it is law you want is not *just* to say something about enforcement. It surely is also to say something about the formal characteristics of the normative order you have in mind as well (Pirie 2013). As I have said, though satisfaction of Fuller's formal criteria clearly aren't sufficient to identify a legal system, his view that gross violation of them collectively means that we are not dealing with a legal system does seem plausible. Any full account would also have to consider the special significance of adjudicatory institutions, real or possible, for legal orders – even

---

[11] Though my brief discussion of global administrative law aimed merely to provide a case study to help us think about the issue of enforcement, it is perhaps worth commenting on another question raised by the possibility of a new law of global governance. That is whether it would be better for legal entrepreneurs to advocate a new kind of law beyond the state or rather an expanded understanding of legal sources within the existing system of international law. The reason the first can seem appropriate is that although the subjects of international law already include not just states, but also institutions and individuals, its sources are held to be found solely in the conduct of states. The evidence that advocates present to support their claim that a new law regulating global governance is emerging concerns primarily institutional practices. This cannot, at present, support an argument that a new set of rules of customary law is emerging (see Kingsbury 2009). No doubt acceptance of an expansion of the relevant range of practices that could ground customary international law is a tall order as a practical matter. But the advantages of that route as opposed to the emergence of a new, separate, global legal order, whose relationship with international law would need to be negotiated, are very great. A revised understanding of customary international law would bring the new legal rules of global governance into an existing legal system of great scope and institutional development that would in turn strengthen, for reasons mentioned in the discussion of fragmentation, the normative claims of the new law.

if you can have law without courts, they are rather central to most legal systems. And much else besides. My aim here is by no means to attempt a full account of the nature of legal normative orders. (I'm not sure that such a classificatory project is particularly important, just for its own sake.) Rather the focus has been on the significance of enforcement in particular, as that is so salient an issue for law beyond the state.

As it turns out, it seems that we can make good on the commonsense idea that law has got something to do with the exercise of power without having to go near the disastrous idea that no person or institution or state is subject to law unless it is subject to an actually existing higher power.

International Responsibility

International law already provides for a measure of enforcement through countermeasures, and further feasible modes of enforcement of global law may emerge. Enforcement means sanctioning the noncomplying legal subject. But do the burdens of those sanctions fall on the right people?

The subjects of global law include individuals, organizations of various kinds, and states. There is no puzzle about the legal and moral obligations individuals have under international criminal law, nor about the moral responsibility of those who fail to comply. (There are questions about the legitimacy of international criminal trial and punishment, but that is a different matter.) But when it comes to corporate entities such as states and international organizations, it is sometimes suggested that neither obligation nor responsibility make any sense. Only people can have duties; only people can be responsible for violating them.

There is actually no puzzle about abstract entities having legal or moral obligations. The obvious analogy here is to corporations. Corporations don't have minds, so cannot deliberate about whether to comply with law or do the right thing, but the management and membership certainly can. Likewise, the people with decision-making authority in the governments of states and the governing bodies of international organizations can choose whether to comply with law. These abstract entities comply (or not) with their obligations through the decisions of their officials.

It is crucial to this commonsense story that there be some institutionalized mechanism for making decisions. We cannot in any meaningful sense say that Christians, as a group, have an obligation not to violate the rights of non-Christians. It is not the group but each individual that has that obligation. But we can talk about the obligations of the Catholic Church, with its officials and decision-making procedures.

There is also no puzzle about responsibility. Responsibility for violations of international law by a state lies with the officials who made the decision. There is no metaphysical puzzle here.

But what about the rest of us, the ordinary citizens; are we also responsible? Suppose I vote for the party that promises to comply with international law, but that it loses to the noncompliance party. I am not responsible for subsequent violations of international law committed by my government. What about those who voted for the noncompliance party? We may say that that they together (in the sense discussed in the previous chapter) are responsible for any violations that were explicitly promised in the campaign – such as a promise to wage an illegal war. But merely voting for a candidate who later violates law does not make anyone responsible for those decisions. So in the vast run of cases, private citizens cannot be said to be morally responsible for acts of noncompliance by their state; responsibility lies entirely with those officials who made the relevant decisions.

Since legally wrongful acts by a state may attract sanctions that will burden the entire population of the state, some have seen a serious problem here. Here is Antonio Cassese:

> The international community is so primitive that the archaic concept of collective responsibility still prevails. Where States breach an international rule, the whole collectivity to which the individual State official belongs, who materially infringed that rule, bears responsibility.[12]

---

[12] Cassese (2005, 241), quoted in Crawford and Watkins (2010, 289). Crawford and Watkins and my companion piece (Murphy 2010), on which this section draws, discuss these issues in more depth than I can here.

Now one possible response to this objection is to offer an account of states as constituting political communities in some strong sense that would make sense of genuine collective responsibility.[13] Such an account would extend responsibility for a state's action even to those citizens who did everything in their power to prevent it. Dworkin's theory of associative obligations and the role of law in forming a genuinely fraternal political community, discussed in the previous chapter, would be one possibility (see also Nagel 2005). I do not find such accounts plausible even as descriptions of an ideal, but we can in any case leave them aside. In our actual nonideal world, probably no state satisfies the strong preconditions of domestic justice required for the kind of community in which all are plausibly thought responsible for the activities of their leaders (Murphy 2010).

The fact is that individuals in most states most of the time are not responsible in any meaningful sense for the particular decisions made by their leaders. But it doesn't seem to me that international law and practice suggest otherwise. The better way to put Cassese's objection is this: given that it is the leaders who make decisions who are morally responsible, and not the public at large or officials assuming office subsequently, it is objectionable that those decisions can generate sanctions that affect the whole population and whose effects can survive a change of government.

Exactly the same objection can be raised about states' contractual liability in cases of "odious debt." Loans taken out by one government, no matter how corruptly spent, must nonetheless be repaid after a change of regime, and the burdens will typically fall on everyone (see Howse 2007; Pogge 2002, 112–15).

Now of course it is also true that both liability to sanction and contractual liability on the part of individuals can burden other nonresponsible

---

[13] By genuine collective responsibility, I mean a responsibility that flows just from being a member of some group. Cases where "we together" do something, discussed in the previous chapter, where the aggregate effect of all our actions is significant though the effect of each act taken alone is morally insignificant, can be understood without appeal to collective responsibility in this sense.

individuals, such as family members. This raises a prima facie objection that is not different in kind to the one we are considering for state responsibility. But the problem is starker in the case of state responsibility because there is not even the attempt to concentrate the burdens on the responsible officials.

In the actual world, where states do not overlap with communities within which genuine collective responsibility might make sense, the justification for making states rather than government officials the subjects of law and the targets of sanctions is going to have to be instrumental. If states are sanctioned for noncomplying actions taken by particular officials, people with no responsibility for those decisions will inevitably incur burdens that they in no sense deserve. The challenge is to show that these kinds of burdens are outweighed by the relative advantage, in terms of good effects, that the current system of state responsibility has over feasible alternatives.

Note that the burdens imposed on people because of the wrongful acts of officials of their states are typically financial. They are not in the nature of punishment, nor do they rise to the level of rights violations (Crawford & Watkins 2010; Murphy 2010). The burdens of state contractual responsibility or responsibility for wrongful acts may be significant, but so too may be the advantages of the state system.

But this does not mean that the state system cannot be made more sophisticated, to distribute these burdens more fairly and provide better incentives to government officials. The state system and the law of state responsibility, as well as the whole international financial architecture within which loan contracts are enforced, could in principle allow for the lifting of the state veil in certain circumstances (Murphy 2010).

The law of the responsibility of international organizations is currently a matter of controversy. The ILC's recent draft articles on the responsibility of international organizations have not been received with unanimous praise (for a survey, see McRae 2012). The problem any law of responsibility for international organizations must face is the same as the problem any kind of justificatory account faces – there are a great many very different kinds of international organizations, with different legal bases, different kinds of affiliations with states, different kinds of impacts on the global scene. The overall question is what the best feasible legal regime would be with regard to legal liability of nonstate organizations; it seems likely that the answer to this question will have many parts. Structurally, the issue is the same as that discussed for states: Why and how would it be justified to impose burdens on people in the form of liability for the decisions made by officers of various international organizations? But it is not as if there are states and just one other kind of organization – there are an unlimited number of possibly relevant distinctions to be made among international organizations. Needless to say, I cannot venture an opinion on where work on this important issue is likely to come out.

The Duty to Obey Global Law

The duty of states to obey international law, or of any subject to obey any kind of global law, is instrumental; subjects should obey when it will do good, and because it will.

Among the deontological arguments for a duty to obey domestic law discussed in the previous chapter, the argument from democratic process and associative obligations evidently would fare worse in the global than the national context.

However, the consent argument fares better, at least for international law. This is because, unlike in the domestic case, it can at least be argued with a straight face that states are not subject to international obligations that they have not expressly consented to. In the case of customary law, the argument relies on the doctrine of the persistent objector. Despite the fact that objecting is no doubt onerous, to infer implicit consent from the failure to object is hardly absurd in the context of the relations among states, not to be compared to Locke's idea that my presence on the king's highway counts as implicit consent.

The doctrine of the persistent objector may itself not be terribly secure (Thirlway 2006, 127). But there are other elements of international legal doctrine that in the end clearly undermine the claim that international law imposes no obligation without consent. There is the idea of *jus cogens*, preemptory law that states cannot contract out of. More secure doctrinally speaking is the exception Hart focused on in his discussion of this issue: new states are taken to be subject to customary law as it exists at the time they come into existence. Last, international organizations such as the Security Council have taken on legislative roles that were arguably never anticipated in the original treaties.

In any event, the factual basis of the consent argument has never been its gravest weakness. The more important point is that there is more at stake with the global legal order than that the valuable practice of honoring international commitments should be supported. It is true that this is a valuable practice, both for each state and for people collectively. But just as the moral stakes of a president's compliance with law are hardly exhausted by the fact that he took an oath of office, there are much stronger reasons for a state to comply with international law than those that flow from any promise or expression of consent.

Another way to bring out the point is to recall the distinction between treaties and soft-law agreements. If consent is the basis for the duty to obey, it applies equally in both cases. Since this is not the way participants in the system think of it, something has gone wrong. Of course soft-law agreements impose obligations; the basis of that obligation is the importance of the practice of making and keeping international agreements. But something more is going on with the obligation to obey the law.

Though consent is not the ground of states' obligations to obey international law, the fact that most states have in fact consented to most of international law is, nonetheless, very important. The moral significance of the fact of consent lies not with its generation of a duty to obey, but in providing an element of accountability (Buchanan and Keohane 2006). Of course, lawmaking by way of treaty is hardly to be thought of as a globally democratic legislative process, but the possibility of a state refusing to sign up adds considerably to the legitimacy of calling noncompliers to account and applying sanctions. The role of consent in international law is thus politically very significant, even though it is not the basis of states' duty to obey.

In the case of domestic law, the basis of the obligation to obey the law, where it exists, is the political obligation to support the institutions of the state. In the case of international law, the obligation is to support the practice of general compliance with the law (see Buchanan 2007, 293–9). That general compliance (supposing the content of the law isn't too bad) is generally speaking good seems hard to deny. International humanitarian law has arguably been enormously important in disciplining the conduct of war. To have a settled law of the sea that is usually complied with, even if it is less than fully just, is clearly preferable to having no law of the sea at all. Similarly the content of international environmental law is hardly what it needs to be, but to have international environmental law at all is a precondition of having good law. It wouldn't be a wise strategy to refuse to comply until law with the right content came about, since other states will have different views about what content is right.

In the case of individual subjects of domestic law, as we saw, the fact that general compliance is better than general noncompliance does not translate into an instrumental duty of obedience to all law all the time. But in the case of international law, it comes close to doing that. In part this is because of the weakness of the enforcement mechanisms available in international law. The more compliance is in effect voluntary, the more harm noncompliance may do. But it is also just a matter of numbers. The situation is not as stark as the one I described for domestic law that applies to branches of government, where only one person or body may be the subject of the law. But there are very few states, relatively speaking, and individual acts of noncompliance by one or a handful of the two hundred odd states could and can make a very significant difference to the practice of compliance. It would seem to be especially important that states that can get away with illegality in self-interested terms should comply. The signal that noncompliance by powerful states sends – that only the weak or the foolish would follow the law if noncompliance were better in self-interested terms – is particularly destructive.

The moral case for compliance with international law, then, is very simple. With so few legal subjects, each act of noncompliance has a reasonable chance of being part of pattern of increasing noncompliance that snowballs into a situation where compliance is no longer the norm. The fact that, if Guzman is right, self-interest usually counsels compliance does not undermine this point. For the lower the overall level of compliance, the less considerations of reputation and so on will counsel compliance on self-interested grounds. Those who argue that there is never a moral duty for states to obey international law must believe that a world without international law would be as good as a world with it. They must believe that the world goes no worse if each state decides for itself what seems right and proper, rather than constraining itself to shared standards of conduct while trying to improve the content of those standards. It goes without saying that the current content of international law and the process of its making both fall way short of feasible alternatives. But to say that states should comply with international law as it now is because that will make the world better need involve no illusions about our nonideal world and is fully compatible with the content of the law being bad enough in a particular case that the benefits of noncompliance outweigh the harms.

Though the reasons are quite different for domestic and international law, and though the case is stronger for domestic law, we here vindicate the idea that law for states typically has stronger moral force than what is usually the case for domestic law applying to individual subjects. As for global law applying to nonstate institutions, the structure of the argument just outlined for international law would apply, though with many important differences. Without attempting to do justice to the details, we can say that the reason for any international organization to comply with law that applies to it will turn on the value of general compliance and the impact on that particular organization's noncompliance.

"Positivism" and "Natural Law" in International Legal Theory

In this book, I have used "positivism" in the way it is generally used in contemporary legal philosophy, to label the view that the grounds of law are always only matters of fact. Within contemporary international legal theory, however, it has other, more expansive, meanings; in particular, it is frequently associated with *voluntarism*, the view that the content of international law flows from states' consent.

A canonical statement of the voluntarist view was made by the Permanent Court of International Justice in the *Lotus* case in 1927: "The rules of law binding upon States ... emanate from their own free will." As Hart (1994, 224–6) pointed out, if we read such a statement as being about the very sources of law, it is confused. Leaving aside the complications of customary law for now, it mischaracterizes even the law of treaties. It is true that no state is bound to a treaty without its consent. But that it is a rule of law that states perform their treaty obligations is not itself a matter of states' wills. No state consented to *pacta sunt servanda* being a legal principle.

Voluntarism about the very sources of international law makes no sense, but there is a better way to interpret this view: the sources of international law being what they are, legal requirements are never imposed on states without their consent. My guess is that most defenders of voluntarism would be content to rephrase their position in this way. The claim is false, as we have seen (though perhaps it once was true), but it is perfectly coherent and it is not absurd to wish that it were (still) true.

Though neither version of voluntarism is implied by the idea that the grounds of law are matters of fact, there are a number of historical and political reasons the two views have been associated. Grotius distinguished natural law from civil law and explained that the latter, unlike the former, was voluntary, grounded in acts of will; the law of nations was a branch of civil law. Thus for Grotius we have, on the one hand, morality or natural law, and on the other hand norms that are derived from acts of will. This suggests that if international law is distinct from morality, it is grounded in acts of will.

Positivist legal theory until the early twentieth century in effect agreed, since the source of law was found in the command of the sovereign. And German "statutory positivism" of the late nineteenth and early twentieth centuries insisted that law is what has been "set down" (*gesetzt*) by an act of legislative will. It is not until Hart that a version of positivism that is completely free of voluntarism emerges.

There is also a political connection, since voluntarism goes along with a traditional view of state sovereignty that is also naturally hostile to the possibility that someone's idea of morality would become a source of legal duties. Thus it is that "positivism" about international law acquired a bad political odor in some circles, which can come as something of a surprise for a newcomer.

It is obviously preferable to keep the two ideas entirely distinct – as Prosper Weil did in his celebrated 1982 defense of a traditional sovereignty-centered view of international law against the inroads of ideas such as *jus cogens*. Weil defended both voluntarism and positivism, which for him was just the view that the grounds of law in international law are matters of fact.

Understanding the use of "natural law" in international legal theory also requires some care. Like other early modern writers, Grotius was not terribly concerned to mark the boundary between morality and positive law. But the contemporary issue is the role of morality in determining the content of the positive or human law. As we saw in Chapter 2, there is no "natural law" theory of the grounds of law; no one thinks that the positive law just is what morality requires, or even that any conflict with morality renders a legal norm invalid. The relevant contrasting view is nonpositivism, the view that legal interpretation will always require moral judgment – most plausibly in the manner of the "moral reading" interpretation of legal materials developed by Dworkin.

A positivist approach and the moral reading will potentially yield different conclusions across the range of international legal sources. The divergence is perhaps most obvious in the context of the interpretation of treaties. Thus a reading of the UN Charter that does not involve moral judgment has it that the NATO bombing of Kosovo in 1999 was illegal as it was neither authorized by the Security Council nor an act of self-defense. As Koskenniemi (2002, 162) reports, most international lawyers have taken the view that though probably morally justified, the NATO action was illegal. A moral reading could certainly find material to work with to reach the opposite legal conclusion. Taking the overall purpose of the establishment of the United Nations to be the securing of peace, the prevention of slaughter, and the protection of human rights, and acknowledging the legitimacy deficits of the Security Council, and so on, it would not be too hard to reach the conclusion that the NATO campaign was legal after all.[14]

The moral reading could also yield different results in the interpretation of the content of customary legal rules. Moreover, and more interesting, it could affect the doctrine of *opinio juris*, such that the moral appeal of the proposed rule could affect the determination of whether there is a sufficient *opinio juris* (see Tasioulas 2007).

I will not here rehearse my argument from Chapter 6 that the standoff between positivists and nonpositivists reflects fundamental differences of belief about the nature of law, and that no compelling argument is likely to be available to move one side closer to another. I will just note that the instrumental political case in favor of positivism is clearer in the case of international law than in domestic law, wherever it may be found (see Kingsbury 2003). Even if we reject crude claims of sovereignty – "no one can tell us what to do" – it is clearly an advantage, if fidelity to law is desirable, to be able to present the content of international law as simply a matter of fact, rather than in part determined by the truth about international right and wrong. Disagreement about the content of that truth is even more obvious globally than domestically, and the accusation that, in practice, this just imposes the opinions of those from powerful states

---

[14] For Dworkin's own, much more detailed and subtle argument, see Dworkin 2013.

is rather plausible. Nonetheless, the instrumental argument fails for the reasons I set out in Chapter 6, most importantly because it only works if it works – that is, if it brings about a convergence in views about the grounds of law – and it is clearly not going to do that.

So on the question of the grounds of international law we are left in the same place as for domestic law. There will be considerable overlap between the two approaches, especially outside the areas of human rights and humanitarian law. We are not left always having to say that according to positivistic law the answer is this, to nonpositivistic law the answer is that. But there will be a range of cases, in the nature of things typically very contentious cases, where the two approaches will yield different conclusions.

9   Conclusion: What Matters?

The discussion of calls for new law in the previous chapter suggests that the question of what makes a normative order a legal order rather than something else matters. To say that "there ought to be a law against it" cannot just mean that someone should stop it, but neither can it mean just that it is wrong or that people should believe it is wrong. It seems worth reflecting on just what we are asking for when we say that.

Of course, if we never in fact needed to know the content of the law in force – if, that is, eliminativism about the law were the right view to take – then we would have no good reason to call for a new law, or a new kind of law. We should rather call for new kinds of institutions and practices of various kinds, and better ways of understanding the moral responsibility of those who occupy various roles within those structures. So eliminativism would render both kinds of question about the nature of law empty.

I have rejected eliminativism. I believe we do need to know the content of the law in force, most importantly because we often have moral reason to comply with law. State officials typically have very strong moral reason to comply with law. It matters what the law is, and therefore the dispute over the grounds of law matters.

But that dispute seems to be in a strange condition. I have claimed that no argument is in sight to move the discussion about the grounds of law forward. I have also argued that this does not matter very much because the two positions agree in very many cases about the factors relevant to determining the content of law. Am I not saying both that the dispute matters and that it doesn't?

In Chapter 5, I distinguished two ways a dispute over the nature of something might matter. The first is that it might be important to come up with an answer. On this way of mattering, I have in effect said that in the area of overlap between positivism and nonpositivism, the dispute doesn't matter very much. But what about the area where the two positions disagree about the factors relevant to determining the content of the law in force? Here the dispute matters and the standoff I see between the two sides seems regrettable. I have not, of course, proved that no new argument will ever reengage and open the minds ·of the participants in the debate. After all, there are some equally intractable debates within moral theory. Some utilitarians will never believe that it is, in principle rather than for pragmatic reasons, wrong to kill one to save five; no one thinks that this means we should give up on moral argument. It's true that the array of relevant factors that can engage the mind in moral discussion is so much richer than in the case of the debate about the grounds of law; one is much more likely to throw up one's hands in a dispute about what law is than in one about right and wrong. But I have not shown that this is the only reasonable response.

Be that as it may, we are left with an important practical problem. I have said that state officials, at least, typically have strong moral reasons to comply with law. What are they to do when the legal issue does not fall into the overlap between positivism and nonpositivism?[1] If it is a single official making the decision, and she has a view about how to figure out what the law provides, then she will proceed accordingly. But where we have disagreement about how to figure out what the law is, problems emerge. Senior foreign office officials are debating the possible bombing of Kosovo. One argues that it is legally permitted; the other that it is not, but that, even after taking into account the moral force of the law, all things considered it ought to be done. The one argues that it really can't

---

[1] I am indebted to Timothy Fowler for pressing this question.

be the case that it is illegal but morally all right, the other replies that of course it can (see Dworkin 2013). They will get bogged down here. And over a dispute that, at this retail level, really doesn't matter. What matters is that the right moral decision gets made about what to do – taking into account not just the facts on the ground, but the content of legal materials both domestic and international and the moral force those materials should have for the entity to which they are addressed. Which means that, for this discussion of an issue that does not fall within the overlap between positivism and the moral reading of law, it is not necessary to first reach some conclusion about the content of the law. It is not necessary, and it would be counterproductive to try.

Here then, is truth in eliminativism. For certain particular decisions, ignoring the law altogether is a good idea. This does not vindicate eliminativism, however, for the reasons laid out in Chapter 6. It is true that any particular moral decision about what to do in light of the legal materials (or, if you like, the political history of the relevant polity) can be made without forming a view about the content of the law. And in some cases, it's better to proceed that way. But the suggestion that therefore we can drop the idea of the law in force from our social conceptual scheme is extremely artificial. In particular, when lawmakers produce legal materials, they think that they are making law, precisely, and it is hard to see how they could go forward with any other self-understanding.

The second way a dispute over the nature of something might matter lies in the domain (broadly speaking) of the critique of ideology. As explained in Chapter 5, we need to know that there are different views abroad about what democracy, liberty, and the rule of law are because we need to be able to uncover rhetorical and ideological maneuvering. The same is true for different views about the grounds of law. The generally dispiriting public discourse about judicial nominations in the United States provides a good example. All sides claim that the nominees they favor will apply the law, not make it, and that the nominees that they do not favor will do the opposite. "Legislating from the bench" is out. But then, judges appealing to their own judgments of political morality in the course of making a decision is also out. There is in the United States no determinate settled law governing adjudication in hard cases, or the force of horizontal stare decisis, so at the very least appellate judges must engage in moral reflection to decide how to go forward when the legal materials do not provide a simple answer. This inescapable point, however, is almost always disavowed in the public sphere. To the extent that politicians defend asking questions about the political views of judicial nominees, they usually suggest that this is needed to smoke out extremists who will make law, not apply it. This game of cat and mouse rather obviously obscures what is really at stake.

If the question concerns the proper weight of precedent, or when a court should depart from the plain meaning of a statutory text, and the relevant legal norms about stare decisis and statutory interpretation do not settle the matter, it is obviously nonsensical to answer by saying that judges should apply the law. But this answer is equally empty if the question is what judges should do in hard cases, especially cases involving interpretation of broad statements of rights in constitutions – for disagreement about whether moral considerations are among the grounds of law maps precisely onto the different camps in that debate.

As Duncan Kennedy (1998) argues at length, the combination of the obvious fact that policy or ideological considerations are inevitably involved in legal decision making in a legal system like that in the United States and the almost unanimous official and professional denial of this fact does great damage to our general understanding of the role of courts in government. More than that, this denial can be described as ideological in that it "increases the appearance of naturalness, necessity, and relative justice of the status quo, whatever it may be, over what would prevail in a more transparent regime"(2). The fact that there are two fundamentally different views about the grounds of law about helps to allow all sides to insist in good conscience that all they ask is that judges apply the law; this shores up the situation of denial. It does so by blocking direct political discussion of what legal decision makers should do, in the system they work within and with the materials they have. Just as with the political values discussed in Chapter 5, then, disagreement about law does open up space for ideological sleights of hand and obfuscation.

So though it isn't generally true that we can simply leave discussion of law aside and talk about something else, here is another context in which that would be the right thing to do. When it comes to judicial nominations, especially for the highest courts, we should ask judges which kinds of considerations they believe a judge may legitimately take into account when resolving legal disputes. As we saw in Chapter 2, judges can give us their theory of adjudication while leaving the issue of the grounds of law open.

There are many other important issues of institutional design that can be fully and better debated while leaving the issue of the grounds of law to one side. Should the legal materials consist more of formally realizable rules, or is it better to make use of broad standards? It is a distraction to argue against standards by saying, for example, that they would allow judges to "make law." What matters in this context is how far we think it is better to tie judges' hands, and how far it is better to leave room for independent judgment.

It certainly matters that we understand both our disputes about the nature of law; we need to know what someone might be trying to slip past us in argument. And both disputes about the nature of law also matter in the first way of mattering – it would be good to have an answer.

Still, sometimes it is better to talk about something else.

References

Ackerman, Bruce. 2010. *The Decline and Fall of the American Republic.* Cambridge, MA: Harvard University Press.

Adler, Matthew. 2006. "Popular Constitutionalism and the Rule of Recognition." *Northwestern University Law Review,* **100**: 719–805.

Adler, Matthew, and Kenneth Einar Himma. 2009. *The Rule of Recognition and the U.S. Constitution.* New York: Oxford University Press.

Alexander, Larry, and Frederick Schauer. 1997. "On Extrajudicial Constitutional Interpretation." *Harvard Law Review* **110**: 1359–87.

Alexy, Robert. 2002. *The Argument from Injustice: A Reply to Legal Positivism.* Oxford: Oxford University Press.

Alston, Philip. 2002. "Resisting the Merger and Acquisition of Human Rights by Trade Law: A Reply to Petersmann." *European Journal of International Law* **13**: 815–44.

Alvarez, Jose. 2005. *International Organizations as Law-Makers.* Oxford: Oxford University Press.

——— 2008. "The Factors Driving and Constraining the Incorporation of International Law into WTO Adjudication." In *The WTO: Governance, Dispute Settlement, and Developing Countries,* edited by Merit E. Janow, Victoria Donaldson, and Alan Yanovich, 611–34. Hunington: Juris Publishing.

Anscombe, Elizabeth. 1990. "On the Source of the Authority of the State." In *Authority,* edited by Joseph Raz, 142–73. New York, New York University Press.

Aquinas, St. Thomas. 1988. *St. Thomas Aquinas on Politics and Ethics,* translated and edited by Paul E. Sigmund. New York and London: Norton.

Aristotle. 1991. *On Rhetoric.* Translated by George A. Kennedy. New York: Oxford University Press.

Austin, John. 1995. *The Province of Jurisprudence Determined*. Cambridge: Cambridge University Press.

Bentham, Jeremy. 1970. *Of Laws in General*, edited by H. L. A. Hart. London: The Athlone Press.

———2010. *Of the Limits of the Penal Branch of Jurisprudence*, edited by Philip Schofield. Oxford: Clarendon Press.

Benvenisti, Eyal, and George Downs. 2007. "The Empire's New Clothes: Political Economy and the Fragmentation of International Law." *Stanford Law Review* **60**: 595–632.

Berlin Isaiah. 1969. "Two Concepts of Liberty." In *Four Essays on Liberty*, 118–72. Oxford: Oxford University Press.

Besson, Samantha. 2010. "Theorizing the Sources of International Law." In Besson and John Tasioulas, 163–86.

Besson, Samantha, and John Tasioulas, eds. 2010. *The Philosophy of International Law*. Oxford: Oxford University Press.

Bix, Brian H. 2005. "Raz, Authority, and Conceptual Analysis." *The American Journal of Jurisprudence* **50**: 311–16.

Blackstone, William. 1765–9. *Commentaries on the Laws of England*.

Brink, David O. 1988. "Legal Theory, Legal Interpretation, and Judicial Review." *Philosophy & Public Affairs* **17**: 105–48.

Brunnée, Jutta, and Stephen Toope. 2010. *Legitimacy and Legality in International Law: An Interactional Account*. Cambridge: Cambridge University Press.

Buchanan, Allen. 2007. *Justice, Legitimacy, and Self-Determination: Moral Foundations for International Law*. Oxford: Oxford University Press.

Buchanan, Allen, and Robert O. Keohane. 2006. "The Legitimacy of Global Governance Institutions." *Ethics and International Affairs* **20**: 405–37.

Burke-White, William. 2005. "International Legal Pluralism." *Michigan Journal of International Law* **25**: 963–80.

Campbell, Tom D. 1996. *The Legal Theory of Ethical Positivism*. Brookfield: Dartmouth Publishing.

———2004. *Prescriptive Legal Positivism: Law, Rights and Democracy*. London: Cavendish Publishing.

———2005. "Prescriptive Conceptualism: Comments on Liam Murphy, 'Concepts of Law.'" *Australian Journal of Legal Philosophy* **30**:20–9.

Cardozo, Benjamin. 1921. *The Nature of the Judicial Process*. New Haven, CT: Yale University Press.

Carnap, Rudolf. 1947. *Meaning and Necessity: A Study in Semantics and Modal Logic*. Chicago, IL: The University of Chicago Press.

Cassese, Antonio. 2005. *International Law*. Oxford: Oxford University Press.

Chalmers, David. 2011. "Verbal Disputes." *Philosophical Review* **120**: 515–66.

Christiano, Thomas. 2008. *The Constitution of Equality: Democratic Authority and Its Limits*. Oxford: Oxford University Press.

Cohen, G. A. 2011. "Capitalism, Freedom and the Proletariat." In *On the Currency of Egalitarian Justice and other Essays in Political Philosophy*, edited by Michael Otsuka, 147–65. Princeton, NJ: Princeton University Press.

Coleman, Jules L. 2001a. *The Practice of Principle: In Defence of a Pragmatist Approach to Legal Theory*. Oxford: Oxford University Press.

——— ed. 2001b. *Hart's Postscript: Essays on the Postscript to The Concept of Law*. Oxford: Oxford University Press.

——— 2011. "The Architecture of Jurisprudence." *Yale Law Journal* **121**: 2–80.

Coleman, Jules L., and Ori Simchen. 2003. "Law." *Legal Theory* **9**: 1–41.

Crawford, James, and Penelope Nevill. 2012. "Relations between International Courts and Tribunals: The 'Regime Problem.'" In Young 2012, 235–60.

Crawford, James, and Simon Olleson. 2010. "The Nature and Forms of International Responsibility." In *International Law*, edited by Malcolm D. Evans, 445–72. Oxford: Oxford University Press.

Crawford, James, and Jeremy Watkins. 2010. "International Responsibility." In Besson and Tasioulas 2010, 283–98.

Cruft, Rowan, Matthew H. Kramer, and Mark R. Reiff, eds. 2011. *Crime, Punishment, and Responsibility: The Jurisprudence of Anthony Duff*. Oxford: Oxford University Press.

Davis, Kevin. 2004. "What Can the Rule of Law Variable Tell Us about Rule of Law Reforms?" *Michigan Journal of International Law* **26**:141–61.

De Búrca, Gráinne. 2010. "The EU, the European Court of Justice and the International Legal Order after Kadi." *Harvard International Law Journal* **51**:1–49.

Dickson, Julie. 2001. *Evaluation and Legal Theory*. Oxford: Hart Publishing.

——— 2007. "Is the Rule of Recognition Really a Conventional Rule?" *Oxford Journal of Legal Studies* **27**: 373–401.

—— 2008. "How Many Legal Systems? Some Puzzles Regarding the Identity Conditions of, and Relations between, Legal Systems in the European Union." *Problema* **2**: 9–50.

Duff, R. A. 2007. *Answering for Crime: Responsibility and Liability in the Criminal Law*. Oxford: Hart Publishing.

Dunn, John. 2006. *Democracy: A History*. New York: Atlantic Monthly Press.

Dworkin, Ronald. 1978. *Taking Rights Seriously*. Cambridge, MA: Harvard University Press.

—— 1985. *A Matter of Principle*. Cambridge, MA: Harvard University Press.

—— 1986. *Law's Empire*. Cambridge, MA: Harvard University Press.

—— 1996. *Freedom's Law: The Moral Reading of the American Constitution*. Cambridge, MA: Harvard University Press.

—— 2006. *Justice in Robes*. Cambridge, MA: Harvard University Press.

—— 2011. *Justice for Hedgehogs*. Cambridge, MA: Harvard University Press.

—— 2013. "A New Philosophy for International Law." *Philosophy & Public Affairs* **4**: 2–30.

Dyzenhaus, David. 1997. *Legality and Legitimacy: Carl Schmitt, Hans Kelsen, and Hermann Heller in Weimar*. Oxford: Oxford University Press.

—— 2000. "Form and Substance in the Rule of Law." In *Judicial Review & The Constitution*, edited by Christopher Forsyth, 141–72. Oxford: Hart Publishing.

—— 2006. *The Constitution of Law: Legality in a Time of Emergency*. Cambridge: Cambridge University Press.

—— 2007. "The Rule of Law as the Rule of Liberal Principle." In *Ronald Dworkin*, edited by Arthur Ripstein, 56–81. Cambridge: Cambridge University Press.

—— 2010. *Hard Cases in Wicked Legal Systems: Pathologies of Legality*. 2nd ed. Oxford: Oxford University Press.

—— 2012. "Hobbes on the Authority of Law." In *Hobbes and the Law*, edited by David Dyzenhaus and Thomas Poole, 186–209. Cambridge: Cambridge University Press.

Edmundson, William A. 1998. *Three Anarchical Fallacies: An Essay on Political Authority*. Cambridge: Cambridge University Press.

—— 2004. "State of the Art." *Legal Theory* **10**: 215–59.

—— 2006. "The Virtue of Law-Abidance." *Philosophers' Imprint* **6**: 1–21.

―――2010. "Political Authority, Moral Powers and the Intrinsic Value of Obedience." *Oxford Journal of Legal Studies* **30**: 179–91.

Epstein, Richard. 1979. "Causation and Corrective Justice: A Reply to Two Critics." *Journal of Legal Studies* **8**: 477–504.

Finnis, John. 1967. "Blackstone's Theoretical Intentions." *Natural Law Forum* **12**: 163–83.

―――1980. *Natural Law and Natural Rights*. Oxford: Oxford University Press.

―――1984. "The Authority of Law in the Predicament of Contemporary Social Theory." *Notre Dame Journal of Law, Ethics and Public Policy* **1**: 115–37.

―――1996. "The Truth in Legal Positivism." In *The Autonomy of Law: Essays on Legal Positivism*, edited by Robert P. George, 195–214. Oxford: Oxford University Press.

―――2003. "Law and What I Truly Should Decide." *American Journal of Jurisprudence* **48**:107–29.

Fish, Stanley. 1989. *Doing What Comes Naturally: Change, Rhetoric, and the Practice of Theory in Literary & Legal Studies*. Durham, NC: Duke University Press.

Fodor, Jerry. 2004. "Water's Water Everywhere." Review of *Kripke: Names, Necessity and Identity* by Christopher Hughes. *London Review of Books*, October 21, 17–19.

Fuller, Lon. 1969. *The Morality of Law*. New Haven, CT: Yale University Press.

Gallie, W. B. 1955. "Essentially Contested Concepts." *Proceedings of the Aristotelian Society* **56**: 167–98.

Gardner, John. 2001. "Legal Positivism: 5 1/2 Myths." *American Journal of Jurisprudence* **46**:199–227.

―――2012. "How Law Claims, What Law Claims." In *Institutionalized Reason: The Jurisprudence of Robert Alexy*, edited by Matthias Klatt, 29–44. Oxford: Oxford University Press.

Garzón Valdés, Ernesto. 1998. "Two Models of Legal Validity: Hans Kelsen and Francisco Suárez." In Paulson and Paulson, 1998, 263–72.

Goldsmith, Jack, and Daryl Levinson. 2009. "Law for States: International Law, Constitutional Law, Public Law." *Harvard Law Review* **122**: 1791–1868.

Goldsmith, Jack L., and Eric A. Posner. 2005. *The Limits of International Law*. New York: Oxford University Press.

Golove, David. 2005–6. "Leaving Customary International Law Where It Is: Goldsmith and Posner's The Limits of International Law." *Georgia Journal of International and Comparative Law* **34**:333–77.

Green, Leslie. 1988. *The Authority of the State*. Oxford: Oxford University Press.

—— 1999. "Positivism and Conventionalism." *Canadian Journal of Law and Jurisprudence* **12**: 35–52.

—— 2010. "Law as a Means." In *The Hart-Fuller Debate in the Twenty-First Century*, edited by Peter Cane, 169–87. Oxford: Hart Publishing.

Greenawalt, Kent. 1989. *Conflicts of Law and Morality*. Oxford: Oxford University Press.

Greenberg, Mark. 2011. "The Standard Picture and Its Discontents." In *Oxford Studies in Philosophy of Law: Volume 1*, edited by Leslie Green and Brian Leiter, 39–106. Oxford: Oxford University Press.

Guzman, Andrew T. 2002. "A Compliance-Based Theory of International Law." *California Law Review* **90**: 1826–87.

—— 2008. *How International Law Works: A Rational Choice Theory*. New York: Oxford University Press.

Habermas, Jürgen. 1996. *Between Facts and Norms: Contributions to a Discourse Theory of Law and Democracy*. Translated by William Rehg. Cambridge, MA: MIT Press.

Hand, Learned. 1952. "How Far Is a Judge Free in Rendering a Decision," in *The Spirit of Liberty: Papers and Addresses of Learned Hand* 103–10. New York: Knopf.

Hare, R. M. 1982. *Moral Thinking: Its Levels, Method, and Point*. Oxford: Oxford University Press.

Hart, H. L. A. 1958. "Positivism and the Separation of Law and Morals." *Harvard Law Review* **71** (1958): 593–629. Reprinted in Hart 1984, 49–87.

—— 1982. *Essays on Bentham*. Oxford: Oxford University Press.

—— 1984. *Essays in Jurisprudence and Philosophy*. Oxford: Oxford University Press.

—— 1994. *The Concept of Law*. 2nd ed. Oxford: Oxford University Press.

Hathaway, Oona, and Scott J. Shapiro. 2011. "Outcasting: Enforcement in Domestic and International Law." *Yale Law Journal* **121**: 252–349.

Henkin, Louis. 1979. *How Nations Behave*. 2nd ed. New York: Columbia University Press.

Hill, Thomas. 2002. "Questions about Kant's Opposition to Revolution." *The Journal of Value Inquiry* **36**: 283–98.

Himma, Kenneth. 2002. "Inclusive Legal Positivism." In *The Oxford Handbook of Jurisprudence and Philosophy of Law*, edited by Jules Coleman and Scott Shapiro, 125–65. Oxford: Oxford University Press.

Hobbes, Thomas. 1651. *Leviathan*.

——— (1681) 1971. *A Dialogue between a Philosopher and a Student of the Common Laws of England*, edited by Joseph Cropsey. Chicago, IL: The University of Chicago Press.

Howse, Robert. 2007. "The Concept of Odious Debt in Public International Law." United Nations Conference on Trade and Development Discussion Paper, No. 185. http://unctad.org/en/Docs/osgdp20074_en.pdf.

Howse, Robert, and Ruti Teitel. 2010. "Beyond Compliance: Rethinking Why International Law Really Matters." *Global Policy* 1: 127–36.

Holmes, Oliver Wendell, Jr. 1897. "The Path of the Law," *Harvard Law Review* 10: 457–78.

Hume, David. 1978. 2nd ed. *A Treatise of Human Nature*, edited by L.A. Selby-Bigge, 2nd ed. revised by P. H. Nidditch. Oxford: Oxford University Press.

——— 1994. "Of the Original Contract." In David Hume, "Political Writings," edited by Stuart D. Warner and Donald W. Livingston, 164–81.

International Law Commission. 2006a. "Conclusions of the work of the Study Group on the Fragmentation of International Law: Difficulties Arising from the Diversification and Expansion of International Law." UN Doc. A/61/10, para. 251.

——— 2006b. "Fragmentation of International Law: Difficulties Arising from the Diversification and Expansion of International Law," Report of the Study Group of the International Law Commission, Finalized by Martti Koskenniemi. UN Doc. A/CN.4/L.682.

Jackson, Frank. 1998. *From Metaphysics to Ethics: In Defense of Conceptual Analysis*. Oxford: Oxford University Press.

Kant, Immanuel. 1996. *The Metaphysics of Morals*, edited by Mary Gregor. Cambridge: Cambridge University Press.

Kelsen, Hans. 1928. "Natural Law Doctrine and Legal Positivism." Reprinted in Kelsen 2006, 391–446.

——— 1967. *Pure Theory of Law*. 2nd ed. Berkeley: University of California Press.

——— 1973. "Law and Morality." In *Essays in Legal and Moral Philosophy*, edited by Ota Weinberger and translated by Peter Heath, 83–94. Dordrecht: Reidel.

———2000. "On the Essence and Value of Democracy." In *Weimar: A Jurisprudence of Crisis*, edited by Arthur Jacobson and Bernhard Schlink, translated by Belinda Cooper, 84–109. Berkeley: University of California Press.

———2006. *General Theory of Law and State*. New Brunswick, NJ: Transaction Publishers.

Kennedy, Duncan. 1976. "Form and Substance in Private Law Adjudication." *Harvard Law Review* **89**:1685–1778.

———1998. *A Critique of Adjudication (Fin de siècle)*. Cambridge, MA: Harvard University Press.

Kingsbury, Benedict. 1999. "Foreword: Is the Proliferation of International Courts and Tribunals a Systemic Problem?" *New York University Journal of International Law and Politics* **31**:679–96.

———2003. "Legal Positivism as Normative Politics: International Society, Balance of Power and Lassa Oppenheim's Positive International Law." In *East Asian and European Perspectives on International Law*, edited by Michael Stolleis and Masaharu Yanagihara, 139–78. Baden-Baden: Nomos.

———2009. "The Concept of Law in Global Administrative Law." *European Journal of International Law* **20**: 23–57.

Kingsbury, Benedict, Nico Krisch, and Richard Stewart. 2005. "The Emergence of Global Administrative Law." *Law and Contemporary Problems* **68**: 15–61.

Koh, Harold Hongju. 1997. "Why Do Nations Obey International Law?" *Yale Law Journal* **106**: 2599–2695.

Kornhauser, Lewis. 2004. "Governance Structures, Legal Systems, and the Concept of Law." *Chicago-Kent Law Review* **79**: 355–81.

———Unpublished Manuscript. "Designing Collegial Courts." Last revised 2012. Adobe pdf file.

Koskenniemi, Martti. 2002. "The Lady Doth Protest Too Much: Kosovo and the Return to Ethics in International Law." *Modern Law Review* **65**: 159–75.

———2012. "Hegemonic Regimes." In Young 2012, 305–324.

Koskenniemi, Martti, and Päivi Leino. 2002. "Fragmentation of International Law? Postmodern Anxieties." *Leiden Journal of International Law* **15**: 553–79.

Kramer, Matthew. 2003. *In Defense of Legal Positivism: Law without Trimmings*. Oxford: Oxford University Press.

Kripke, Saul. 1980. *Naming and Necessity*. Cambridge, MA: Harvard University Press.

Kumm, Mattias. 2005. "The Jurisprudence of Constitutional Conflict: Constitutional Supremacy in Europe before and after the Constitutional Treaty," *European Law Journal* **11**: 262–307.

———2012. "The Moral Point of Constitutional Pluralism: Defining the Domain of Legitimate Institutional Civil Disobedience and Conscientious Objection." In *Philosophical Foundations of European Union Law*, edited by Julie Dickson and Pavlos Eleftheriadis, 216–46. Oxford: Oxford University Press.

Lacey, Nicola. 2006. *A life of H.L.A. Hart: The Nightmare and the Nobel Dream*. Oxford: Oxford University Press.

Lamond, Grant. 2001. "Coercion and the Nature of Law." *Legal Theory* **7**: 35–57.

Lefkowitz, David. 2004. "Legitimate Political Authority and the Duty of Those Subject to It: A Critique of Edmundson." *Law and Philosophy* **23**: 399–435.

———2008. "(Dis)solving the Chronological Paradox in Customary International Law: A Hartian Approach." *The Canadian Journal of Law and Jurisprudence* **21**: 129–48.

Levinson, Daryl. 2011. "Parchment and Politics." *Harvard Law Review* **124**: 657–746.

Lieberman, David. 1989. *The Province of Legislation Determined: Legal Theory in Eighteen-century Britain*. Cambridge: Cambridge University Press.

Mackie, J. L. 1974. "What Is De Re Modality?" *Journal of Philosophy* **71**:551–61.

Marmor, Andrei. 2009. *Social Conventions: From Language to Law*. Princeton, NJ: Princeton University Press.

———2010. "The Pure Theory of Law." In *The Stanford Encyclopedia of Philosophy* (Fall 2010 Edition), edited by Edward N. Zalta. http://plato.stanford.edu/archives/fall2010/entries/lawphil-theory/.

———2011. *Philosophy of Law*. Princeton, NJ: Princeton University Press.

McRae, Donald. 2012. "The Work of the International Law Commission, 2007–2011: Progress and Prospects." *The American Journal of International Law* **106**: 322–40.

Morrison, Trevor W. 2010. "Stare Decisis in the Office of Legal Counsel." *Columbia Law Review* **110**: 1448–1525.

Murphy, Liam. 2001a. "The Political Question of the Concept of Law." In
Coleman 2001b, 371–409.

—— 2001b. "Beneficence, Law, and Liberty: The Case of Required Rescue."
Georgetown Law Journal **89**: 605–65.

—— 2005. "Concepts of Law." *Australian Journal of Legal Philosophy*
30:1–19.

—— 2007. "Razian Concepts." *American Philosophical Association Newsletter
on Philosophy and Law* **6**: 27–31.

—— 2008. "Better to See Law This Way." *New York University Law Review*
83: 1088–1108.

—— 2010. "International Responsibility." In Besson and John Tasioulas,
299–320.

Murphy, Liam, and Thomas Nagel. 2002. *The Myth of Ownership: Taxes and
Justice*. New York: Oxford University Press.

Nagel, Thomas. 2005. "The Problem of Global Justice." *Philosophy & Public
Affairs* **33**: 113–47.

Nozick, Robert. 1974. *Anarchy, State, and Utopia*. New York: Basic Books.

Parfit, Derek. 1984. *Reasons and Persons*. Oxford: Oxford University Press.

Paulson, Stanley L. 1998. "Introduction." In Paulson and Paulson 1998,
xxiii–liii.

—— 2006. "On the Background and Significance of Gustav Radbruch's Post-
War Papers." *Oxford Journal of Legal Studies* **26**: 17–40.

Paulson, Stanley L., and Bonnie Litschewski Paulson, eds. 1998. *Normativity
and Norms: Critical Perspectives on Kelsenian Themes*. Oxford: Oxford
University Press.

Pauwelyn, Joost. 2003. *Conflict of Norms in Public International Law –
How WTO Law Relates to Other Rules of International Law*. New York:
Cambridge University Press.

Payandeh, Merhdad. 2011. "The Concept of International Law in the
Jurisprudence of HLA Hart." *European Journal of International Law* **21**:
967–95.

Perry, Stephen. 1987. "Judicial Obligation, Precedent, and the Common Law."
Oxford Journal of Legal Studies **7**: 215–57.

—— 2001. "Hart's Methodological Positivism." In Coleman 2001b, 311–54.

—— 2009. "Where All Have the Powers Gone: Hartian Rules of Recognition,
Noncognitivsm, and the Constitutional and Jurisprudential Foundations of
Law." In Adler and Himma 2009, 295–326.

——2013. "Political Authority and Political Obligation." In *Oxford Studies in Philosophy of Law: Volume 2*, edited by Leslie Green and Brian Leiter, 1–73. Oxford: Oxford University Press.

Pirie, Fernanda. 2010. "Law before Government: Ideology and Aspiration." *Oxford Journal of Legal Studies* **30**: 207–28.

——2013. *The Anthropology of Law*. Oxford: Oxford University Press.

Pogge, Thomas. 2002. *World Poverty and Human Rights: Cosmopolitan Responsibilities and Reforms*. Cambridge: Polity Press.

Posner, Eric, and Adrian Vermuele. 2011. *The Executive Unbound: After the Madisonian Republic*. New York: Oxford University Press.

Posner, Richard. 2008. *How Judges Think*. Cambridge, MA: Harvard University Press.

Postema, Gerald. 1986. *Bentham and the Common Law Tradition*. New York: Oxford University Press.

——2012. "Legal Positivism: Early Foundations." In *The Routledge Companion to Philosophy of Law*, edited by Andrei Marmor, 31–47. New York: Routledge.

Putnam, Hilary. 1975. "The Meaning of 'Meaning.'" In *Mind, Language, and Reality: Philosophical Papers, Volume 2*, 215–71. Cambridge: Cambridge University Press.

Radbruch, Gustav. 2006. "Statutory Lawlessness and Supra-Statutory Law." Translated by Bonnie Litschewski Paulson and Stanley L. Paulson. *Oxford Journal of Legal Studies* **26**: 1–11.

Railton, Peter. 1984. "Alienation, Consequentialism, and the Demands of Morality." *Philosophy & Public Affairs* **13**: 134–71.

Rawls, John. 1996. *Political Liberalism*. New York: Columbia University Press.

——1999. *A Theory of Justice*. Revised edition. Cambridge, MA: Harvard University Press.

Raz, Joseph. 1979. *The Authority of Law: Essays on Law and Morality*. Oxford: Oxford University Press.

——1980. 2nd ed. *The Concept of a Legal System: An Introduction to the Theory of Legal System*. Oxford: Oxford University Press.

——1985. "Authority and Justification." *Philosophy & Public Affairs* **14**: 3–29.

——1986. "Dworkin: A New Link in the Chain." *California Law Review* **74**: 1103–19.

—— 1988. *The Morality of Freedom*. Oxford: Oxford University Press.

—— 1993. "H. L. A. Hart (1907–1992)." *Utilitas* **5**:145–56.

—— 1994. *Ethics in the Public Domain: Essays in the Morality of Law and Politics*. Oxford: Oxford University Press.

—— 1999. *Practical Reason and Norms*. 2nd ed. Oxford: Oxford University Press.

—— 2001. "Two Views of the Nature of the Theory of Law." In Coleman 2001b, 1–38.

—— 2004. "Incorporation by Law." *Legal Theory* **10**:1–17.

—— 2005. "Can There Be a Theory of Law?" In *The Blackwell Guide to the Philosophy of Law and Legal Theory*, edited by Martin P. Golding and William A. Edmundson, 324–42. Malden: Blackwell Publishing.

Ripstein, Arthur. 2009. *Force and Freedom: Kant's Legal and Political Philosophy*. Cambridge, MA: Harvard University Press.

Roberts, Simon. 2005. "After Government? On Representing Law without the State." *Modern Law Review*, **68**:1–24.

Rundle, Kristen. 2012. *Forms Liberate: Reclaiming the Jurisprudence of Lon L Fuller*. Oxford: Hart Publishing.

Scalia, Antonin. 1998. *A Matter of Interpretation: Federal Courts and the Law*, edited by Amy Gutmann. Princeton, NJ: Princeton University Press.

Scanlon, T. M. 1998. *What We Owe to Each Other*. Cambridge, MA: Harvard University Press.

Schauer, Frederick. 1991. *Playing by the Rules: A Philosophical Examination of Rule-based Decision Making in Law and in Life*. Oxford: Oxford University Press.

—— 2005. "The Social Construction of the Concept of Law: A Reply to Julie Dickson." *Oxford Journal of Legal Studies* **25**: 493–501.

—— 2010a. "Was Austin Right After All? On the Role of Sanctions in a Theory of Law." *Ratio Juris* **23**: 1–21.

—— 2010b. "When and How (If at All) Does Law Constrain Official Action?" *Georgia Law Review* **44**: 769–801.

—— 2012. "The Political Risk (If Any) of Breaking The Law." *Journal of Legal Analysis* **4**: 83–101.

Segal, Gabriel M. A. 2004. "Reference, Causal Powers, Externalist Intuitions and Unicorns." In *The Externalist Challenge*, edited by Richard Schantz, 329–46. Berlin: Walter de Gruyter.

Shapiro, Scott. 2011. *Legality*. Cambridge, MA: Harvard University Press.

Shklar, Judith N. 1998. *Political Thought and Political Thinkers*, edited by Stanley Hoffmann. Chicago, IL: University of Chicago Press.

Sidgwick, Henry. 1982. *The Methods of Ethics*. Indianapolis, IN: Hackett Publishing.

—— 2000. "Bentham and Benthamism in Politics and Ethics." In *Essays on Ethics and Method*, edited by Marcus G. Singer, 195–218. Oxford: Oxford University Press.

Simmons A. John. 1979. *Moral Principles and Political Obligations*. Princeton, NJ: Princeton University Press.

—— 2001. *Justification and Legitimacy*. Cambridge: Cambridge University Press.

—— 2005. "The Duty to Obey and our Natural Moral Duties." In Wellman and Simmons, 93–196.

Simmons, Beth. 2010. "Treaty Compliance and Violation." *Annual Review of Political Science* **13**: 273–96.

Smith, Stephen A. 2011. "Normativity of Private Law." *Oxford Journal of Legal Studies* **31**: 215–42.

Soper, Philip. 1984. *A Theory of Law*. Cambridge, MA: Harvard University Press.

—— 2002. *The Ethics of Deference: Learning from Law's Morals*. Cambridge: Cambridge University Press.

—— 2007. "In Defense of Classical Natural Law in Legal Theory: Why Unjust Law Is No Law at All." *The Canadian Journal of Law and Jurisprudence* **20**: 201–23.

Stavropoulos, Nicos. 1996. *Objectivity in Law*. Oxford: Oxford University Press.

—— 2003. "Interpretivist Theories of Law." In *The Stanford Encyclopedia of Philosophy* (Fall 2008 Edition), edited by Edward N. Zalta. http://plato.stanford.edu/archives/fall2008/entries/law-interpretivist/.

—— 2014 Forthcoming. "Legal Interpretivism." In The Stanford Encyclopedia of Philosophy, edited by Edward N. Zalta, <http://plato.stanford.edu>.

Tamanaha, Brian. 2001. *A General Jurisprudence of Law and Society*. Oxford: Oxford University Press.

Tasioulas, John. 2007. "Customary International Law and the Quest for Global Justice." In *The Nature of Customary Law: Philosophical, Historical and Legal Perspectives*, edited by Amanda Perreau-Saussine and James B. Murphy, 307–35. Cambridge: Cambridge University Press.

Thirlway, Hugh. 2006. "The Sources of International Law." In *International Law*, 2nd ed., edited by Malcolm D. Evans, 115–40. Oxford: Oxford University Press.

Twining, William. 2003. "A Post-Westphalian Conception of Law." *Law and Society Review* **37**:199–258.

——2009. *General Jurisprudence: Understanding Law from a Global Perspective*. Cambridge: Cambridge University Press.

von Bogdandy, Armin, Philipp Dann, and Matthias Goldmann. 2008. "Developing the Publicness of Public International Law: Towards a Legal Framework for Global Governance Activities." *German Law Journal* **9**: 1375–1400.

Waldron, Jeremy. 1996. "Kant's Legal Positivism," *Harvard Law Review* **109**: 1535–66.

——1999. "Special Ties and Natural Duties." In *The Duty to Obey the Law: Selected Philosophical Readings*, edited by William A. Edmundson, 271–99. Lanham, MD: Rowman & Littlefield Publishers.

——2001. "Normative (or Ethical) Positivism." In Coleman 2001b, 410–34.

——2002. "Is the Rule of Law an Essentially Contested Concept (in Florida)?" *Law and Philosophy* **21**: 137–64.

——2007. "Legislation and the Rule of Law." *Legisprudence* **1**: 91–124.

——2008. "The Concept and the Rule of Law." *Georgia Law Review* **43**: 1–61.

——2009a. "Can There Be a Democratic Jurisprudence?" *Emory Law Journal* **58**: 675–712.

——2009b. "Who Needs Rules of Recognition?" In Adler and Himma 2009, 327–49.

Walker, Neil, and Grainne de Burca. 2007. "Reconceiving Law & New Governance." *Columbia Journal of European Law* **13**:519–37.

Waluchow, Wilfrid J. 1994. *Inclusive Legal Positivism*. Oxford: Oxford University Press.

Weil, Prosper. 1983. "Towards Relative Normativity in International Law?" *The American Journal of International Law* **77**:413–42.

Weinberg, Jonathan, Shaun Nichols, and Stephen Stich. 2001. "Normativity and Epistemic Intuitions," *Philosophical Topics* **29**: 429–60.

Wellman, Christopher Heath. 2005. "Samaritanism and the Duty to Obey the Law." In Wellman and Simmons 2005, 3–89.

Wellman, Christopher Heath, and A. John Simmons. 2005. *Is There a Duty to Obey the Law?*. Cambridge: Cambridge University Press.

Whittington, Keith E. 2009. *Political Foundations of Judicial Supremacy: The Presidency, the Supreme Court, and Constitutional Leadership in U.S. History*. Princeton, NJ: Princeton University Press.

Williams, Glanville. 1945. "International Law and the Controversy Concerning the word 'Law.'" *The British Year Book of International Law* **22**: 146–63.

Yankah, Ekow. 2008. "The Force of Law: The Role of Coercion in Legal Normativity." *University of Richmond Law Review* **42**: 1195–1255.

Young, Margaret A, ed. 2012. *Regime Interaction in International Law: Facing Fragmentation*. Cambridge: Cambridge University Press.

Index